The Heart of the Community

The Heart of the Community
The Best of the Carnegie Newsletter

Edited by
Paul Taylor

NEW STAR BOOKS

VANCOUVER

2003

New Star Books Ltd.
107 - 3477 Commercial Street
Vancouver, BC   V5N 4E8
www.NewStarBooks.com
info@NewStarBooks.com

Printed and bound in Canada
First printing June 2003

Publication of this work is made possible by grants from the Canada Council, the British Columbia Arts Council, and the Department of Canadian Heritage Book Publishing Industry Development Program.

NATIONAL LIBRARY OF CANADA CATALOGUING IN PUBLICATION DATA

Main entry under title:
  Heart of the community : the best of the Carnegie newsletter / Paul Taylor, editor.

  ISBN 0-921586-94-9
  1. Canadian literature (English) — British Columbia — Vancouver.* I. Taylor, Paul, 1952–
PS8257.V35H42 2003   C810.8'0971133   C2003-910557-1
PR9198.3.V3H42 2003

This book is dedicated to Harold David

Contents

READING THE STREETS: 1998

ORDINARY EVERYDAY EVENTS: 1999

Introduction

The *Carnegie Newsletter* began in the early summer of 1986, with Al Mettrick hired on a UI Top-up program to start it. After walking around and saying "I'm Al and I'd like you to help me make a newsletter" the first issue came out on August 15 — 12 pages in 60 copies made on a copier upstairs.

It's covered issues like poverty, housing, safety, the sex-trade, free trade, community gardens, the community cornered by developers, gentrification, homelessness, drugs, alcohol, volunteers, kids, sports, foodlines and more.

The *Newsletter* has been razed as a slimy, yellow rag; vilified by many local wannabees for getting too close to the truth of what such were about or after.

Like life, there are no final solutions or resolutions to the many issues and problems and exciting events covered herein. What this book attempts to do is present some of the good contributions that have appeared over the years. A lot of stuff is necessarily tied to the facts or events at a particular time and just to give a context would take more than the reprint; the essence of the stories and poetry herein often transcend the timeliness of a particular piece.

A final note — the Carnegie Newsletter has always been done, with the exception of the actual printing, by volunteers. That alone is truly amazing.

PAULR TAYLOR
VOLUNTEER EDITOR

The Contents of the *Newsletter* Itself

The skeletal picture following is not a history of Carnegie; it doesn't even pretend to cover the myriad events, drama cum outrageous comedy of forces affecting and permeating life in the Downtown Eastside / Vancouver / BC / Canada / North America / Earth / . . . Maybe the reason for putting such short shorts here is just to allow some stereotypical constructs which any readers of an actual *Newsletter* know barely scratch the surface. Decisions made in corporate boardrooms about moving business to the lowest-wage dictatorship in Central America or Asia certainly affect single parents having to feed their children and perhaps becoming another of the women murdered or missing and treated as a statistic in the Downtown Eastside . . .

An editor can make magic happen, can weave a thread through seemingly unconnected selections and hope the reader ties into it.

1986 Finding stories, people getting inspired by seeing and sharing their experiences and poetry, internal struggles at Carnegie Centre and opposing forces, backgrounded by Expo 86. Carnegie, as a community centre, is six years old.

1987   Downtown Eastside Duck; attempts to kill the newsletter by the besieged board, patrons rally to dissolve board and elect a fresh one, Crab Park opening and access issue, End Legislated Poverty and "Justice. Not Charity" campaign, Publication of *Hastings and Main*, Vander Zalm's vomit.

1988   Poornography, opposition to Free Trade Agreement (FTA), Sheila Baxter's first book *No Way To Live: Poor Women Speak Out*, Larry Loyie's play *No XYA*, poverty and politics, "When I give food to the poor, they call me a saint. When I ask why the poor have no food, they call me a communist" — Dom Helder Camara.

1989   Development / NPA / Gordon Campbell / Socreds / Vander Zalm, Evelyne Saller honoured, more on FTA, Yanum Spath's generosity, War on the Poor, hello to CEEDS, community groups bill Claude Richmond for excessive disorder caused by "find work or starve" notice, Campbell's campaign promises . . . promises, "Starve a Socred, Feed a Child," Downtown Eastside Poets.

1990   Garry Gust's *Subjective Alloys*, *Help in the Downtown Eastside* (free resource guide), front steps called Cocaine Corner, PROUT, GST, ELP and street kids, VanderZalm and *Les Miserables*, Oppenheimer Park gets year-round staff, questions on women disappearing.

1991   Sheila's *Under the Viaduct: Homeless in Beautiful BC* published, negative decision on Gitksan-Wet'-suwet'en case, Action Canada Network,

issues of perceived inequities at First United Church, *Newsletter* marks five years, *Help in the Downtown Eastside* gets complete translations into Spanish and French by volunteers, Poverty Is Violence Against Children.

1992   La Boussole opens, Tenants' Survival Guide, reality of five-week month reaches daily press, NDP forms government, concerns about DERA answered with housecleaning (real boats rock), ACN and NAFTA, ELP and Taste of the Nation, battered women and growing cynicism, East Timor.

1993   DERA welcomes Barb Daniel, Mulroney goes down in flames, Joan Smallwood says "welfare close to collapse," Diane MacKenzie starts working on Gathering Place, trip to Nicaragua, waterfront "realms," drugs and overdoses, feds out of housing, Woodward's closes.

1994   Alcan and Native rights, social safety net unravelling, ginseng brandy, national "debt clock" used for business propaganda, Crab Park overpass shot down after seven years of chicanery, call for restricted hours on "convenience" stores, Four Corners Community Savings, Sandy Cameron's 24-part series on history of DTES and Carnegie, fight against casino, overdoses.

1995   Sandy's *Fight for Community* published, Incredible Shrinking Neighbourhood as never-before-heard-of "neighbourhoods" created, condo vice, Woodward's, Bud Osborn publishes *Lonesome Monsters*, Gastown Groupies & Woodward's, Speaking in Chalks,

Gustafsen Lake, John Shayler and the return of Tinseltown, Gathering Place opens, In The Dumpster.

1996   Women's Memorial March, kids & sex, Canada Assistance Plan killed and poor blamed, suite size vs. condos, Friends of DERA stupidity gets Bruce Eriksen back to help, Carnegie Community Action Project, court condemns Friends of DERA as being malicious, vexatious and totally without merit, *Newsletter* is ten years strong.

1997   Sam Roddan begins association with *Newsletter*, Kevin Annett and allegations of murder and theft in Port Alberni, Kassem Aghtai and Woodward's, apartheid in Canada, association with women in Burnaby Correctional Centre for Women, treatment and addiction, Walls of Change.

1998   Gentrification, the Big Lie, drug crisis and user centre, cooking and rice wine, *Taking Another Look at Class,* essays by Sandy Cameron, poornography and drug use, beginnings of Carnegie's Street Program.

1999   Humanities 101, net loss of housing and permission to control conversions / demolitions unused by city, CCTV (surveillance via closed-circuit television), fight to keep Dave Dickson, so-called Community Alliance, Carnegie's CD crew, police and *Through a Blue Lens.*

2000   Diane Wood and cover art, Tinseltown / International Village and accusations of discrimination, hep-C, poor laws and Gastown, Vision Quest, WTO, four-pillar approach, municipal strike closes Carnegie until patrons rally, Libby's re-election and Mason Loh.

2001   Listening Post, *Poor Bashing: The Politics of Exclusion* by Jean Swanson, Community Alliance, Woodward's, and their "enforcement-only" approach to drugs, street mosaics, FTAA, violence against women, Campbell / Coell and the lies, September 11, "hate literature," American flag with stars replaced by corporate logos, The Dugout.

Acknowledgements

Al Mettrick, who got it going; Cindy Carson, Nancy Jennings, Diane MacKenzie and other staff who recognized the awesome potential, Charlie at Budget for doing it right, and finally to all the volunteers who wrote poetry and articles, drew graphics or cut up old magazines, did layout, editing, collated, stapled, folded and distributed it. Eternal thanks to you, gentle reader, for your input and energy and help in making *Ye Olde Carnegie Newsletter* a gem, a jewel of the Downtown Eastside. Thanks to PEACH (Partners for Economic and Community Help) for the funding to enable this book to be.

Efforts have been made to contact all living contributors to this book. By our very nature, some authors use pseudonyms, some have no fixed or known address and some are only known to still be on the planet when they stop by. Both the Carnegie Community Centre Association and Partners for Economic And Community Help (PEACH) disclaim favour for the articles, graphics and poetry contained herein. New Star Books will undoubtedly put its own disclaimer in to cover everybody's ass.

Special thanks to Sandy Cameron and Dan Feeney for wisdom, expertise and creativity. Artwork is mostly by Tora, Garry Gust, Wing Ko, Sam Roddan and Diane Wood. The mosaic incorporated in the cover design is by Marguerite T.

YOUR POLITICS STINK

1986

Well, It's Not Fancy

Well, it's not fancy, but this is the first issue of a new paper for Carnegie people, by Carnegie people. We have no money but that's OK. What we do have are people . . . the best kind of people, nearly 150 of you using the place every hour of every day. One hundred and fifty stories an hour. A goldmine! When we get rolling it'll be the best little paper in town.

ALAN METTRICK
15/8/86

The Poet's Task

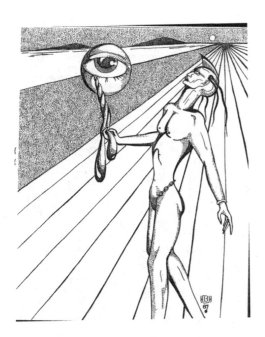

If language
is culture,
is communication,
is universe,
is everything,
it's urgent
I listen
to the words I use.

CLAUDIUS IVAN PLANIDIN
1/11/86

The Poor Are an Embarrassment

The poor are an embarrassment to the rich. We're just too different. We always show up at the door expecting to get in free. We complain about the prices — and never seem to wear the right clothes. We just don't know how to carry on a decent conversation about business opportunities in Hong Kong, and even pick butts out of your ash-trays . . . then we have the nerve to tell you your politics stink.

The poor are always embarrassing anyone with enough money in their pockets to cover expenses — and the rich hate us because we always show up at the wrong time and ruin the idea that the good life is enjoyed by all.

It's not so much because we don't have money that we are thrown out of "in" places — it's just that poor people are so goddamned embarrassing to have around.

TORA
1/10/86

Prison Violence

Ever wondered
After rampant rage
Has destroyed cell blocks
And ended lives.
Even when Inmate committees
Have telexed Ottawa
To warn of the pending disaster
It seems then Ottawa is only too ready
After death and chaos
to dispatch officials
To get to the bottom of things
Ever wondered
if work programs were meaningful
If men and women were treated with
    dignity
And respect
It might be different
Ever wondered.

BEVERLY-JEANNE WHITNEY
15/11/86

THE NEWS-PAPERS COULDN'T PRINT IT

1987

'. . . in this place you never know — it's doubtful if you'd find this kind of involvement anywhere else with such un-involvable people.'

— DAVE McCONNELL

Carnegie

Carnegie didn't just happen along
like some flower girl in
the beer parlours smiling
& selling teddy bears.

Years of hard work went into
forcing political dragons
to give up dreaming about
business men's clubs & parking lots.

Years of hard work —
to turn this stone building into
something like sunrise.

Day by day — year by year
Making it happen down here.

I don't know how many people
come & go, or how many hours
Volunteers work to get things done,
or who's responsible for what,
because my mind
doesn't work that way.
But we all take care of business
more or less; sooner or later
we all join hands.

Day by day — year by year
Making it happen down here.

A Centre like this is
Something that holds the outside
    together;
a circle of safety,
a point of communication
for anyone — everyone —
young or old, smart or dumb,
clean or dirty, sane or crazy.
Where else could lifetimes
like these get lived together?

Even when it's only
sharing tobacco or spare change
on the second floor . . .
reading the newspaper on the first
    floor . . .
playing a guitar on the third floor,
in the theatre, on the stairway . . .
Learning to listen
To see each other
To remember the names & faces
of real people in a real neighbourhood.

Day by day — year by year.

No place can be heavier than here
No place can be lighter
At the centre of
Vancouver's basement community
the streetsigns, bars & boring
hotel corridors almost disappear.
Even the cops have to be polite
when they come in here.
People agree to respect one another
but that doesn't stop them

from speaking their minds.
Maybe you'd be surprised . . .
what's on people's minds these days —
the newspapers couldn't print it,
couldn't even tell the whole story.

There's no other community centre
where you're waiting to get in
off the streets as soon as
the door opens every day.

No other community centre
to something like the Downtown
    Eastside.
No other community
building a spaceship like Carnegie —
full of black sheep,
aliens in a neighbourhood of aliens,
a family of aliens
learning to trust one another,
to remember who we are
— who we always were —
at the heart of a community.

The experience of just
opening the door
for every new person
who walks in off the street
with a trust in sober survival.

Survival of social disaster
Survival of personal tragedy
Survival of changes
like Expo & restraint
Survival of urban development
where they try to wipe out
your personal history &
replace it with an answering service.

We are the people — day by day
year by year — we are the people
making it happen down here.

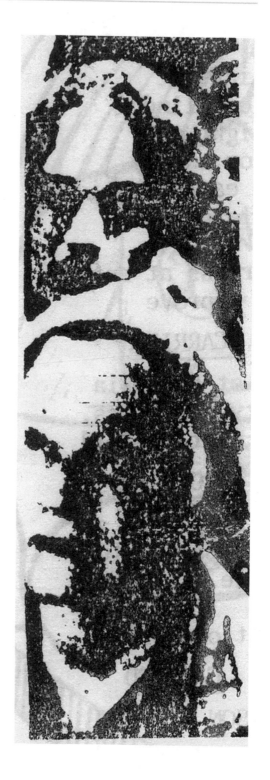

Remembering to keep the traditions of
street survival alive;
the traditions of down-to-earth
    characters,
like the reality of
everyone who walks through the door,
everyone who knows they're sharing
something real in an unreal world.

You want to build a new world
that will fire the imagination
& free the hearts of your children?
Build it around something solid,
something real,
like the Carnegie Centre,
like the Learning Centre,
like waking up with steady hands —
with coffee & communication
in the Cabaret on Tuesdays,
with politics & paint & woodwork
in the basement,
music & technical skills,
reading and writing on the top floor —
with healing encounters,
fascinating characters
crazy contrasts —
growing strong for survival.

Stronger than the welfare freeze
Stronger than booze
Stronger than the rent increase
Stronger than the streetfront
with commercial claws.

At the Centre we're building
an alternative to living alone
At the Centre we're making
a success out of failure.

Day by day — year by year
Growing up all over again
Making it happen down here.

From the ashes of
yesterday's tragedy
burning in the streets —

Climbing out of the dark,
the loser's soul
reaching for something
that's so close
it's already getting true.

Day by day — year by year.

Everyone says
something's happening down here
Everyone's got their own idea
about what's happening too.
But Carnegie's got some kind of
magic with people . . .
Making it happen,
Day by day — year by year
Making it happen down here.

TORA
1/3/87

Beer Glasses Tinkling, People Cursing

Beer glasses tinkling, people cursing,
Sweat dripping off the walls and chairs,
Blues person singing 'bout "Violence
ain't got no conscience, but love do,
    sometimes."

Man saying, woman saying "Watch my
    beer,
I gotta make me some room"
Smoke driftin' in and out of every
shirt and pant slack and sweater,
ashtrays overflowin' — and someone
    says someone
owes him something or other;

Eyes alert, senses hardened and the
    blues person singing
"Some folks live for life, some folks live
    to die."
And the waiter screams, "Another
    round here!"
and everyone wants one more and the
    blues person singing
"If I had a dime for every time I waited

for the morning, alone. I'd own the
    world."
and everyone heard . . . that time
    everyone heard!

DAVE McCONNELL
15/3/87

Dear Readers,

I have learned recently that a very small group of misinformed
people have been spreading a rumour about me. These hopelessly naive fools have apparently been telling other people
that I am a nice guy.

Nothing could be further from the truth. So, to set the
record straight, I wish to state here and now that I am a total
jerk at least 99 percent of the time.

Thank you.

SAM SLANDERS
1/5/87

Ineffable

Abide, moment.

— NIETZSCHE

Though the moon in the city is a much muted moon
She still speaks to me of thoughts lost arriving.
She remembers a night from my childhood in winter
when fat snowflakes fell too softly for words to relate.
I ache for the wonder — oh! paltry word — that fell on me then,
Kissed by the silence of a cool, windless night.
I stood 'neath a sky black with compassion,
alone on the black that circumf'renced my life,
alone in the snow with my heart and the night,
But what my heart knew on that long ago night
With Christmas forgotten in the cool windless night,
The moon will not tell me; and empty words and the moon
are all that remain of that child and that night.
Though the moon in the city is a much muted moon,
She still speaks to me of thoughts lost arriving.

STEVEN BELKIN
1/4/87

Ubiquitous Unicorns

When I left New York, black remnants of snow were being sprayed everywhere by the thousands of cars. It was well below freezing, but that's normal for January, right? Before this flight, any airplane that I'd been on had a maximum time of three hours in the sky, with a movie and people sleeping or reading.

The flight time to India is 20 hours, with two stops for some reason but no getting off. The inside became like a tourist trap after five or six hours; stewardesses and passengers both having goods and souvenirs for sale. Kids were running up and down the aisles until told to sit down and people of every race and creed imaginable were present.

Hello Bombay!

I stepped off the plane into 80-degree weather with the tropical sun beating down — "it was a cool winter." After customs — "Tourist, sir" — and walking outside to get a bus to the train station, I had my first experience with culture shock. Beggars were all over the place, hands out and pointing to their deformities — mangled limbs, open

sores on their faces and bodies, being
blind — and trying to get anything
from the rich air travellers. I had about
$4.50 American, personal worldly
wealth, but it wasn't possible to get that
across to the people pleading with me. I
was a foreigner — must be rich — in
their minds; no one but a rich foreigner
comes to India.

On the trip to the city proper, every
street was lined on both sides with little
four-by-four-foot shops that were hugging the curb and facing the stores on
the main floors of buildings. Pedestrians walked between the double fronts
amid sellers hawking and yelling for
attention to their wares. Outhouse-size
shops usually had one or two items for
sale . . . fruit; grains; pots; pans; cigarettes; books; soft drinks; balls of cow-
shit mixed with straw for starting fires
. . . anything you could think of had a
store to itself.

The trains were booked solid for the
next five days for all points — at the
station were the omnipresent beggars
and about two thousand people with all
their possessions. I took $100 from
money I was carrying for the General
Secretary in Calcutta and bought
another airplane ticket. I'd learned from
an English-speaking Turk that trains in
India have three classes: First Class is
like Canadian railways with stewards
and room and big windows; Second
Class Reserved means being in a car
with 90 others, all bags and goats and
chickens too, and just squeezing in
wherever. (I didn't ask about Third
Class . . .)

In Calcutta, I delivered the money to
the GS, and asked to go on to Varanasi
for training. The Central Office Secre-

tary said that wasn't advisable, since the
lifted government ban on the 26 sections of the organization was still unof-
ficially in effect — even though Ms.
Gandhi was in jail for corruption. A
ticket was purchased for a one-way trip
through the Himalayas to Kathmandu,
Nepal. The training centre there was
still operating and had gotten no overt
pressure to close.

The Himalayas are incredible! As the
Nepalese bus wound its way higher and
higher, people and animals got scarcer.
Nothing else exists but the bus, the
mountains and the sky. Then, fabled
Kathmandu. This is a city of over

100,000 inhabitants, but the picture presented to the West is of a mythical and isolated abode — having only sporadic and wary contact with the outside world. In reality: shops, stores; an open zoo of goats, chickens, cows, llamas, buffalo, elephants; both foot and vehicle traffic; and of course beggars, thieves, con artists, with rape and murder and everything else.

The animals are a trip: as cows are sacred, they can eat anything anywhere — especially off the shelves and benches in storefronts. If you hit one or even yell, you may find an arm that looks just like yours on the ground, as some "devotee" hacks it off with their machete.

Incidentally, the bus travelled for a few miles on the Peking Highway, built and paid for by the Chinese government. This gesture of goodwill also provides a road for tanks and troop carriers if (when) China decides to invade, like in Tibet.

My expectations of the spiritual dropped to almost nil when I saw a near-riot in Ratna Park between the local version of Hare Krishna and who turned out to be their head honchos from HQ in New Delhi. Seems these vicious bastards had come up to whip the locals back into line.

I wandered around the central marketplace and saw a full-grown water buffalo, just slaughtered, with rivers of its blood adding to the garbage in the gutters. This was in an open temple with pictures of their deity, a blue elephant, all over the place. No shit! As I walked down the street to the training centre, a real elephant sauntered by!

When I finally arrived, I had about two bucks left, but the training was free. The teacher expected me to have something, but my delivering the funds to GS in Calcutta had given me a "by." Donations paid for food.

One part of the training is to go for one week begging for all food, saying nothing, buying nothing and being given one clay pot and a box of matches. One cooking session per day and a second meal could only be the cold remains of the first one.

Before leaving, I had acquired dysentery, or chronic diarrhea. The trip to Calcutta was beset with stomach cramps, and a few days after arriving I went blind for a while. At the Central Office, food (rice and veggies) was provided twice a day, but my legs ballooned from water retention, a symptom of severe malnutrition. Body weight was less than 100 pounds but to get money to buy better food and medicine I had to beg in the streets. My vision returned as days passed, and the dysentery was stopped by eating nothing but rice.

When someone comes up to me here and says they're hungry — "Haven't eaten since last night; no meal for another two hours and I'm starving . . ." — it doesn't get much sympathy. Starvation is the daily companion of over a quarter of the people on this planet.

What we have here as basic necessity — guaranteed income, food twice a day at least, free clothes, shelter . . . — an old saying: you don't know what you've got 'til it's gone.

PAUL R TAYLOR
1/4/87

Prison Justice Needs More Than a Day

I had the opportunity to take part in the 11th annual Prison Justice Day activities with Claire Culhane and 11 other people.

Our cavalcade held a vigil at nine prisons. The first one we called at was the Pre-Trial Centre in downtown Vancouver. We walked with placards in front of the centre and prisoners yelled their appreciation of our support while a guard viewed us with binoculars. One of our banners read: "Big Brother is Staring at YOU."

Next on our agenda was a visit to the Deer Lake Resort (Oakalla). We paraded up and down in front of the fence. This antagonized the guard, who immediately herded the inmates back inside like cattle. The guard remarked to us, "See what you've done! Because of you, they have to go inside half an hour earlier." Despite this, the prisoners appreciated our support and did not lose their sense of humour. One said, "Throw the clippers over."

We then went on to the Twin Maples in Maple Ridge, which is a minimum-security prison for women. It is in a farm-like setting and women are allowed to keep their babies with them. Like chickens, the women are only locked up for the night. We had perfect timing here. We arrived just in time to leaflet the visitors who were leaving.

Security was extremely tight at the next two prisons, which are back-to-back in the wilderness near Agassiz. Even though the prisoners were not allowed to see us we still held the vigil in front of the gates.

The security was tight at Mission Prison but we were finally allowed to talk to prisoners over the fence at Ferndale. This was the highlight of our tour and the inmates thoroughly enjoyed visitors from the outside.

The last prison on our tour was the Regional Psychiatric Centre in Matsqui. While we held our vigil in front of the gates an ambulance drove in complete with sirens to take one of the prisoners to the hospital.

Claire Culhane is currently prohibited from visiting prisons in BC (being an outspoken and articulate critic!) and is going to court on September 10 to challenge this and get an order, under the Charter of Rights, so she is allowed to visit British Columbia prisons. She is not forbidden to visit prisons anywhere else in Canada. We hear through the "grapevine" that the government would like this matter settled out of court.

We came home exhausted but well satisfied with our day. There was a beautiful sunset as we drove down the highway to Vancouver.

IRENE SCHMIDT

15/8/87

My Favourite Whore

My favourite whore
gave me a glass
of Canada Cooler on
the street last night.
She said, "Don't worry,
I'm the only one
who's been on it."

I thought about AIDS
but I drank it anyway
I thought too

about the use of condoms . . .
And perhaps the next time

I kiss a woman anywhere . . .
I'll use Saran Wrap — and
pretend she's a sandwich.

But when I went back
in the bar
to sing another set of songs . . .
And forgot about AIDS,
Whores . . .
and I don't care if I
do die, do die, do die . . .

TOM LEWIS
15/9/87

A Place Is a Place Is a Place . . .

For us all: wages, unemployment insurance, pensions, GAIN aren't rising equally with rents. Sure, everything costs more, but we figure that landlords should learn to control themselves.

Damn near every place you go into the rent has gone up in the last six months but no one talks about it for fear of eviction. Government subsidized incomes are either the same or less, but the costs continue to rise for rent, food, medical care, gas, bus fare, prescription drugs, etc. etc. ETC. . .

CRAB PARK OPENING 1987

GUARDIAN of the Harbour
by Tom

What we have is an unbalanced and unstable society. We are not bleeding hearts; we are not crying wolf . . . we are simply stating facts. People seem to think that things will get better as if by magic, but unless we make changes to the way things are — to the status quo — things will get much worse.

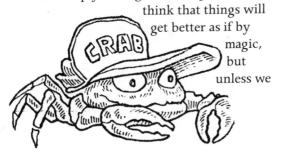

People have a right to good housing, the same as we have a right to good medical care or services or whatever. It isn't a privilege for the privileged, it's a right for everyone.

DAVE MCCONNELL
1/6/87

JOHN
GETTING
TRICKED

1988

The Balmoral's Cockroach

In a Balmoral room
    the cockroach creeps
In and out of cracks
Looking for a place to lay
    her many tiny eggs.

She climbs into the pocket
    of a john getting tricked
and returns with him
    to Shaughnessy
:to live with his wife and kids.

SHEILA BAXTER
(1/3/88)

Dad

I know life is not always easy for you,
Although it's not easy being the
    daughter
of a wonderful father.

We've had some bad, good and joyful
    times.
But I'll always treasure the good times.

When I'm with you — you make me
    feel special.
But when we're miles apart I feel the
    loss
of your laughter and your wonderful
    stories.

Dad, I just want you to know
you're always in my thoughts, mind and
most of all, in my heart.

I love you Dad.

Happy Father's Day.

LOVE ALWAYS, MARGARET
(1/6/88)

Big Buck the Porn Pimp Talks to the Fraser Committee

*Red Hot Video testified before the
Fraser Committee on Pornography and
Prostitution. The courts had found
them guilty of distributing videos
depicting the rape and torture of
women as erotic entertainment. The
essence of their defense:*

I wan' my rights!
I wan' freedom of expression!
I wan' Tits 'n' Ass!
I wanna see a vagina ripped by a
    meathook . . .
I wanna see rip rip rip
rape rape rape . . .
I stand on my right to freedom of
    choice.
I stand on boobs, melons, tits, knockers,
    jugs,
rockets, headlights, HOO-TERS,
ass, cunt, pink, beaver, twat, pussy,
    hole, cherry,
slit, snatch, gash.

See, I'm not putting up with these
    uptight feminists
who can't take a joke.
Piss on 'em. Shit on 'em. Chain 'em.
Whip 'em. Rape 'em.
That'll learn them to contravene my
    right to freedom.
I want my rights to freedom of choice.
My, my, my, my, MMMM-YYYYY
    freedom of choice.
Cut their boobs off, cut off
those melons, tits, knockers, jugs,
    rockets,
headlights, HOO-TERS.
Kick 'em in the ass, stick a broom
up that cunt, pink, beaver, twat, pussy,
    hole, cherry,
slit, snatch, gash.
That'll learn them!
This is a free country! That's it!

JANCIS M. ANDREWS
(1/3/88)

Don't Let Children Play Hooker

Criminal Code, Section 195(4) reads: Every person, who, in any place, obtains, for consideration, the sexual services of a person who is under the age of eighteen years is guilty of an indictable offence and is liable to imprisonment for a term not exceeding five years.

(1/3/88)

Haiku for a Downtown Eastside Friend

a man of means indeed
 to still have toilet paper so late
 in this five-week month

Cuba Dyer
(1/10/88)

Moral Purpose

Sue Harris has had her finger on the pulse of the Downtown Eastside for years, to stay ahead of the machinations and secret agendas of developers, the big money and the redneck jerks. Since the late 70s Sue has brought her hard-won wisdom and energy to every issue that, if not fought, would bring more disruption and frustration to the lives of thousands of residents.

This isn't a eulogy or a "Superwoman" story: Sue is leaving the Downtown Eastside and BC and Canada — she is moving to England! Part of the reason is not getting the nomination for alderman. Sue won a seat on the Parks Board in 1984 and, her trademark, did superior work for the two-year term. Sue worked for the past two years on community issues; for tenants' rights, welfare problems, for Crab Park and police liaison with us over liquor and pornography and women's rights, for the quality of life for the disadvantaged vis-à-vis safety from robberies and bureaucratic foul-ups, worked for years to have knives made illegal on the streets (the recent ruling to ban knives in pubs was a direct result of Sue's persistence), keeping the problems of Lysol and cooking wine before City Hall . . . and of course more.

We talked a few days ago of the need for "progressive" people to rethink their personal ideologies.

Sue spoke of her sexual orientation during our talk because, she said, "I have to." She cited her being a lesbian as the reason for COPE waffling on her nomination. This kind of doublethink, where people say they support gay rights and the rights of people whose sexual orientation is different from the "norm" (theirs), but retain their subconscious prejudices, is felt all the time by her. She had talked of her personal sexual abuse and the legal action she is taking against her father on a TV show, and feels that this also contributed to her support diminishing. Sue is writing a book to be titled *The Bogeyman Is Real*, which will contain her philosophy on the gaps in peoples' thinking, i.e., if you are in favour of gay rights but cannot even say the word sex or homosexual or lesbian, if you refuse to discuss the reasons for child porn and incest and abuse; if the interrelationships between these and racism and housing and poverty and movies and . . .

Sue Harris wins the grudging admiration of people from all walks of life and of different political persuasions for her persistent clarity on social issues. It bespeaks her inner commitment to an ideology that must include everyone, not just those who share her views. The progressive movement will have a clearer picture due to her admirable constancy of purpose over the last decade — her moral purpose. Go well, Sue.

PAULR TAYLOR
(15/11/88)

Parking Lot, First United Church

In the underground garage
a street person sleeps
in a cardboard box, as if indicating
his own world has ground to a halt
in this place where cars proclaim
another world that's going somewhere.
Caught up by headlights
he hangs from his own high beam
of catatonia, the black light
that swallows the flash
and lash of tongue of those
who protest they've already paid
one loonie
for his six feet of earth.
Welfare recipients
must have a permanent address,
a place to park themselves, and maybe
that is what has drawn him here,
to create a box number
of cardboard and harsh neon and
a cold wind
that does not slow down
but hits hard
as a hand ordering him out.
But he remains motionless, already far
gone into himself, stalled
in his individual defeats,
and curled fetal-like
against a human race that roars by
on a southward or a northward,
an eastward or a westward exodus,
leaving him behind, packed up
and abandoned in a corner
like some inconvenient parcel
left for someone else to find.

JANCIS M. ANDREWS
(15/12/88)

EYEBALL TO EYEBALL

1989

The Philosophy of War

I started at Woodward's
Where the only staff attention I could
     get
Came from a talking Christmas tree
Who asked me what my name was.

Being a boycotter of XMAS, I ignored
     the
Question and went to an underground
     Mall
Where window-shopping is considered
     a
Serious offense against the Capitalist
     system.

Gripping my wallet tightly
I raised my hands in surrender
And walked into a pharmacy that was
Disguised as an over-evolved
Canadian Tire store.

Within minutes I found a whole stack of
Raid roach traps, and with a small urge
To sing the American National anthem,
I purchased one.
I walked home with my weapons
And laid them on the battlefield;
Wiping out a new generation of roaches
Within days.

To Nature, whom I consider the Master
Landlord, I say:
"It's either me or the cockroaches
Who will exist in this cubicle."
Therein lies the philosophy of War.

SKID ROW JOHN
(1/1/89)

Morning Prayer for Today

I am beautiful
Each and every day
I am getting better and better

And I give thanks for my new life
I'm a very special human being
The great spirit loves me

I love the great spirit

I love all things
I belong to the creator

I love you all brothers and sisters
Coming from your brother Terry

TERRY FLAMOND
(15/3/89)

To My Friend Jim, Who Runs the Bar

To my friend Jim, who runs the bar
And John who pulls the beer
I live close by — don't need a car
On Thursday I do come in;
Friday night I'm back to sin.
I do not drive & I do not sling
But oh how I wish I could sing.

— —

I'm not so young but I'm not old
There are times when I get bold
This is the bottom of the page
And we don't come here to talk of age.

This is called recreation
We used to have it in our nation
Now that times are tuff again
Shall I drink or just refrain?
All that matters is the taxes
Vote for Bill or buy from Max's
What you got — take me Jack
Thirty years in a dirty shack.

This is not all that I could say
But this is all — all for today.

DON HODGSON
(15/3/89)

Me as a Volunteer

I really enjoy being a volunteer here at Carnegie. I have been a volunteer for 4 years. I enjoyed it becoming a volunteer because I can learn how to do the job. So far I've done the reception and the concession and started helping on the *Newsletter*.

I hand out tickets and balls and answer phones; also in the pool room and in the coffee shop — which I really like.

I was surprised when I first came to Carnegie and was asked if I wanted to volunteer. I really like it when staff come up to me and ask if I could volunteer here or there. Even if they don't ask, I ask them if I can in places that really need volunteers.

BIRDIE W
(15/12/89)

Doing the Door

It can be dull. Very dull indeed. All you do is stand at the front door or sit and say hello to make sure you get eye contact from patrons coming in. Within seconds you must be able to detect signs of drug or alcohol influence.

Sometimes it's pretty hard with people constantly coming in and out. Usually I try to see them walking up the steps. I don't like it when some guys are really tanked and it's cold outside and late at night.

I remember one night this man had just gotten out of the joint. I guess the first thing he did was go out and have a few beers. He then came to Carnegie and I could tell he was drinking. He asked, "I just got out of jail and all I want to do is read a newspaper. I don't want to cause any trouble . . . just read the paper in peace." I had to tell him that he couldn't come in. He bowed his head and quietly repeated himself. Sue finally came by and told him he had to leave. I didn't have it in me to refuse the guy entrance when he was fresh out of the slammer.

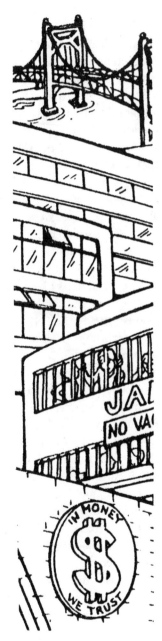

Some people become rather forceful and aggressive. I can recall a few occasions when patrons would curse at the top of their lungs and try to push me aside to get in. They'd be calling me names and threatening to get me when I got off shift. Many times I'm eyeball to eyeball with them and they're slobbering and spitting as they talk. Other times people shake my hand and thank me for not letting them in. They compliment me on a job well done!

When I first started I was warned of the possibility of getting hurt. Around the third or fourth shift I did alone on security, one man I was clearing from the front steps had a bottle of ginseng brandy. He, after I tried talking to him, raised the bottle to forehead level and mumbled some gibberish like, "Are you challenging me to a fight?" I quietly said, "No. I just want you to have fun somewhere else." With that he lowered the bottle and staggered away with his friends. I had to stay calm inside but I was a bit scared too. When people are that drunk they are unpredictable and anything can instigate them to be violent. Fear sometimes keeps me alert.

Then there's the people with heavy problems and I must face it. One young woman who wanted a drug rehab worker was literally screaming, "You don't care about me! You don't give a fuckin' shit if I have to work the streets and sell my body! This place doesn't want to help me! Go to HELL! Whitey!"

I pointed out to her that a man at the Balmoral Hotel hands out syringes. He could've helped her but nothing doing. I was off duty the next day but that incident and testimonies from the Doing Time exhibit upstairs filled my conscience. I saw her near the Brandiz and she had a black eye. I said hello to her but she ignored me. When I see her these days she smiles and at least talks to me.

Other situations like calling an ambulance can be really messy. I remember in August during the PNE there were three stabbings in three nights. All were within feet of the Carnegie walls. I worked the second and third nights. On Thursday night Egor came around midnight with some cinnamon danishes. Paul and I were at the door. Everyone was surprised with the nice gesture. We all went to the front desk and began pigging out. Next thing I knew Gord was telling me that someone had been stabbed and was in the building. It was a strange transition from calm to edgy. Detectives, newspaper reporters and an ambulance crew were surrounding the guy. He was hurt in the chest and stomach. He had been barred but ignored it because of what happened, knowing he could get help.

For someone who had lived 22 years in suburban Ottawa, it was not easy to swallow.

Egor then came again on Friday, near midnight. Again he had danishes and again someone yelled, "Call an ambulance! Some old guy has just been stabbed near the bus stop!"

I ran outside and blood was literally gushing down the sidewalk. This man looked at least 55 years old. His wife was screaming so I let her hold me as the police were not offering much comfort to her. Gord later said with a shrug, "Hey man, you haven't seen shit yet." Right.

Over half an hour later another person was hurt at the Balmoral.

Fortunately it hasn't been that bad of late. I'll tell ya though, if it wasn't for the majority of patrons, I'd give up . . . People like Henry Hebert and Alan Williams and Mike and others keep me going. Doing the door either days or nights means lots of people smiling when I say hello to them. Sometimes young children are about the front steps and I love playing with them. I make a point of cleaning the steps whenever finding them too dirty with butts and coffee cups.

Doing the door also means doing all the patrons who love Carnegie a favour; just trying to keep her clean inside and trying to do a good job. It is certainly not an easy job but it pays off in the long run.

Those front steps though, they've seen a lot . . . and if they could only talk!

STEVE ROSE
(1/4/89)

Song Without Words . . .

for LBF

I wanted to write you some words you'd
    remember
words so alert they'd leap from the page
crawl up your shoulder, lay by your
    ears
and be there to comfort you
down through the years . . .
but
it was cloudy that day and I was lazy
so I stayed in bed just
thinking about it.

I wanted to write you and tell you that
    maybe
love songs from lovers
are unnecessary.
We are what we feel
and writing it down seems foolish
    sometimes
without vocal sound . . .

but
I spent the day drinking coffee
smoking cigarettes and looking in the
    mirror
practicing my smile.

I wanted to write you one last long love
    song

that said what I feel
one final time.
Not comparing your eyes to the stars
but
telling you only
how like yourself you are . . .
but by the time I thought of it
found a pen, put the pen to ink
the ink to paper
you were gone . . .

and so this love song has no words.

ATIBA

(15/4/89)

If Honour Is Truth

If I were a rat in a bucket
instead of your daughter,
would you take up the shovel just once,
killing me outright?

Few are the people whose smiles
I have sought with such rigour,
soaked in, treasured, like the rare pure
    smiles
alighting your face. And now

this long decade later, the distance
between us is finally a comfort,
not devastation. Bad boy, kicking his
    toy-like
offspring around rooms, into corners,

opting for tyranny in the home
instead of the harder inward struggle
that ends at peace. Your mistake lay
in thinking you could escape

dealing directly with your pain.
A bad boy, pushing his fears
and rage onto children, and *mastering*
    them.

For children grow.
Having escaped the confines
of your psyche, and becoming the
    terrifying
outside world, we are approaching.

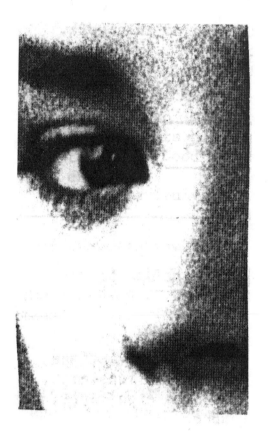

If you were a wild dog
instead of my father,
how many times would I try to befriend
    you,
before shooting you down?

JOANNE ARNOTT
(15/6/89)

It Was the Poetry What Done Me In

See these grey 'airs?
Know what I bin doin'
To earn a few bucks?
Putting up posters!
I ask you — at my time of life!

I coulda been a bleedin stockbroker
Or a corporate whatsit by now.
It was the poetry what done me in.
Shoulda never bin exposed to it
At a tender age.
Sent me off, it did, on a wild goose
    chase
After Truth and Beauty —
Quite forgot about money.

So, 'ere I am
Sticking up ruddy posters

Instead of follering me muse.
Disentitled from UIC
Because I listed me trade
On the form —
POET.
"I am seeking work as a poet."

Disentitled
To a pittance of recompense
By prosy people
Who
Like Plato
Want no Poets
In their Ideal Republic.

DAVID BOUVIER
(1/9/89)

Meditation

O meet it is and sweet it is
To cuddle and to kiss
Though the laws of our society
Crown loving with distress.

O meet it is and sweet it is
For youth and maid to wed
Though the laws of our society
For joys bring griefs instead.

O meet it is and sweet it is
To give birth to girls and boys
Though the laws of our society
Rob families of their joys.

O meet it is and sweet it is
For youth to have its dreams

Though the laws of our society
Damn hopes, gut youth, smash dreams.

O sweet it is, O sweet it is
To see with open eyes
That the laws of our society
Not long can tyrannize.

O sweet it is to join the fight
To set our people free
From the laws of our society
From the bonds of property.

BEA FERNEYHAUGH (1940S)
(15/10/89)

WOLF'S AT THE WINDOW

1990

PROUT

Five fundamental principles of PROUT:

1. No individual should be allowed to accumulate any physical wealth without the clear permission or approval of the collective body.

2. There should be maximum utilization and rational distribution of all mundane, supramundane and spiritual potentialities of the universe.

3. There should be maximum utilization of all physical, metaphysical and spiritual potentialities of unit and collective bodies of the human society.

4. There should be proper adjustment amongst these physical, metaphysical, mundane, supramundane and spiritual utilizations.

5. The method of utilization should vary in accordance with the changes in time, place and person, and these utilizations should be of a progressive nature.

The Progressive Utilization Theory (PROUT) is given for the good & happiness of all.

P.R. SARKAR
(1/2/90)

maybe i shoulda took up drinking

mama christened me alexandra marie but i haven't been called anything like that for years and years

everybody that knows me now just calls me al but there aren't too many around anymore i can call a friend i mean a real friend only what you might call acquaintances i guess like the people who live in this hotel where i got a room on the second floor i was 57 when i moved here and i been in this place five years come the first of february oh i know it's not much of a room but I put my things around and it's kind of homey what i like the best though is the window where i got my chair and i sit here looking out at the parking lot i get to see all the nice new cars parked there and i imagine how it would be if wilf was still alive and we could take one of them cars for a drive to seattle or maybe get on the ferry and go over to the island I could watch those seagulls floating behind the ferry like they do and we could drive to courtenay and I could see how the old place looks

that's where me and wilf came from god more'n 40 years ago when I was 18 and he was 20 we never did own a car and i don't know how to drive anyways but we might have got a secondhand one if wilf hadn't spent most of his pay on drinking and stuff then when he died ten years ago I was left alone and I didn't have no experience in any kind of work except what you do at home wilf never wanted for his wife to work but i wish now I had the kids were real good at first but of course they don't live here any more

so now i don't go out much since I been living here but I do like my win-

dow to be honest about it that's about
all I do like columbia hotel sounds great
eh well it's not so great damn there's
another one of them bugs where's my
shoe who'd have ever thought i'd end

up here all by myself looking out the
window at this stinking parking lot.

ANNE RAYVALS

(1/2/90)

Smithers Secondary School

We received your latest newsletter today, and I wanted to tell you and your staff
how much we enjoy reading it. It gets a great deal of attention from the students
and they have gained from it an altogether new and pretty much unexpected perspective and insight. I believe that our getting your newsletter gives our kids a
valuable opportunity to look out into someone else's world through their eyes.

Because I believe this to be a positive connection for us to continue and to cul-
tivate, I have (just now) asked the principal for the money to get us a subscription for the next year. You'll know if I've been successful if there is a cheque in
this package. I'm writing this letter beforehand because I have the time to do it
now and it is *much* overdue!!!

I also wanted to say that the April visit of the Downtown Eastside Poets has
proven to be the starting point for which I had been searching. My kids have
been writing like mad and they have even agreed to doing a public reading at the
Directed Studies Presentations next month! Again, my thanks for their help and
momentum.

Now I must go to another meeting. Thanks for everything.

LORNE C. THOMPSON

(15/6/90)

The Downtown Eastside Comes Alive

Reprinted from THE VOICE —
*Smithers Secondary School's weekly
newspaper*

A voice that shared another way of life
was heard at our school, Friday
evening, April 6. Four poets, PJ, Cuba
Dyer, Bud Osborn and Margaret, not
only read poetry, but vividly reincar-

nated their thoughts, feelings and past
experiences.

The Downtown Eastside is an area of
Vancouver where frustration, loneliness, hunger and poverty are often part
of daily life. The people who live there
have found a way to express their
thoughts and feelings. They call themselves the Downtown Eastside Poets and

they write directly from their own personal experiences.

Through assistance from the Canada Council Explorations Grant, the poets, who meet at the Carnegie Community Centre, are able to tour throughout BC

Each of the four poets presented their poetry in their own unique ways. PJ was very vocal, almost dynamic and her poems were outspoken and upfront. Cuba was soft spoken and her pieces were about her feelings, her views and her memories. Bud's voice was a captivating monotone as he read comfortably about attempted suicide and life on the streets. Margaret, a new member of the group, spoke honestly and sincerely about her feelings, life, and friendships.

Sitting in the audience, one could easily feel and make the transition from one poet to the next. One student who attended said that the poets showed a whole different side of life in BC and that we should realize just how lucky we really are. Another student liked the fact that the actual authors read their own poems. She said it had a great effect and that it was totally different from the "classroom" experience of poetry. A "non-poet type" as he described himself, felt that it opened doors to new ways of self expression.

It doesn't take five years of university to be able to write a poem. All a person needs is feelings and the desire to express them.

Bud Osborn lives in the Downtown Eastside of Vancouver. Bud was one of the four poets who visited our school a few weeks ago. A lot of his inspiration comes from conversations, actual happenings around him. One of the poems Bud read was "mullin's brother."

mullin was another 50-year-old loser living in a halfway house, but he had something that made him feel good anyway. he wrote perfectly metrical sonnets — hundreds of them — along the lines of elizabeth barret browning, & considered himself a poet without peer. one day mullin was with his brother in the angry-sea-inn, talking about his sonnets, & his brother said, "what's so hard about writing poems nobody wants to read?" "you can't do it," mullin said. "oh yeah?" replied his brother. "never," said mullin. "I'll write a poem right now," his brother said, & peeled the label off his beer bottle, borrowed a pen from mullin, scribbled something, passed it over & said, "here, a poem!" mullin looked at it, read it aloud, & said, "that's not a poem. nobody'd buy that." "I will," said a guy sitting a few stools away. "I'll buy that poem," he said, & handed a dollar bill to mullin's brother, who'd written

— bottles full
bottles empty
dreams

Have a great week!

TRISH ELKIN
(15/6/90)

Condemned

Society says
education
and skills
are most
necessary
I think
sometimes
it kills
Communication
must be more
than that
I

know people
who are scared to speak

cause they don't
talk good
couldn't write
any better
pretty bad —
I had a friend
who killed himself
his people
were very humiliated
on his note
he misspelled
suicide
on his grave
I wrote
George is dead, died
and gone to Hell
'cause he
couldn't spell

N'INGIN SNAPPING TURTLE
(15/7/90)

To All the Great Volunteers

To all the Great Volunteers who helped keep this huge place working all year —
Merry Christmas and a Happy New Year! You all deserve the best for all the wonderful hard work you do. Merry Christmas to the volunteers who are in the hospital or elsewhere. You are all greatly missed. And thank you, volunteers, for
working so hard and standing my many bad moods. I will try harder in the
future to be more appreciative.

JANICE SAUL
(15/12/90)

Sign in the Window

sign on the window
says Learning Front for rent
and you hand me a button
for literacy day and I say
stick it
in your own lapel
while you bury our people
in prisons and psych wards
dump us on park benches
plow us under

with pomp and ceremony
with stacks of glossy PLAC reports
that flame up and burn our eyes
and the heat rises
a growing illumination
that "Five-year blueprint
for literacy in B.C."
was never designed to include us
who are the foundation
the blood and the blueprint

and there's money for
sewers
the drainpipes that
funnel
our blood to Victoria
blood of those crushed
by your edifice of greed
bloodsuckers and
parasites
with your drunken
revelries
in the bowels of the
legislature
drunk on the blood of
the poor
of the dispossessed of
the homeless
of single mothers of
those who work
to support the insatiable

bloodlust
of each sadistic Socred
whose salary sucks up
more each year
than the whole
operation of the
Learning
Front whose head spins
in technicolor
mad dreams of Dracula
Vlad the Impaler, with
genocidal
blueprint then as now.
and hope remains,
then as now
with the Aboriginal,
with the blood
this is pre-literate and
post-literate
with the power of the
majestic "No"
and in this week, festooned with
balloons filled with Victoria hot air
hear the ancient howl of the wolf
as it bursts your balloon
in this land that never was for rent
as we tear down TORA's timeless logo
with the rent sign of your barricaded
soul and the wolf's at the window
and the sign is clear

MIKE KRAMER
(1/9/90)

DOWN HERE

1991

The *Carnegie Newsletter* and the Politics of the Heart

The *Carnegie Newsletter* belongs to the members of the Carnegie Centre. The Carnegie Centre, one of the most-used community centres in Canada, is located in the Downtown Eastside of Vancouver, the city's oldest community, with a residential population of ten thousand citizens.

The newsletter, all 24 to 32 pages of it, is published twice a month. Seven hundred copies are printed, and these are distributed by hand. The paper is free to residents of the Downtown Eastside.

In the *Carnegie Newsletter* the people of the Downtown Eastside are exercising the power to define their own reality. Consider, for example, the following small part of a character sketch by Anne Rayvals about a 62-year-old woman living in a hotel room:

> . . . oh I know it's not much of a room but i put my things around and it's kind of homey what i like the best though is the window where i got my chair and i sit here looking out at the parking lot i get to see all the nice new cars parked there . . . .so now i don't go out much since i been living here but i do like my window to be honest about it that's about all i do like . . . sounds great eh well it's not so great damn there's another one of them bugs where's my shoe who'd have ever thought i'd end up here all by myself looking out the window at this stinking parking lot.

Traditionally the woman in this story has been silent, but now she speaks, and her voice challenges the myth of a just society.

The *Carnegie Newsletter* overflows with the liberating power of self-definition:

Carnegie didn't just happen along
like some flower-girl in
the beer parlour smiling
and selling teddy bears.

Years of hard work went into
forcing political dragons
to give up dreaming about
businessmen's clubs and parking lots.

Years of hard work
to turn this stone building into
something like sunrise.

> *Tora, from his epic poem*
> *"Carnegie"*

There's pain on a voyage of self-discovery. We know that we're not the people they said we were, and we are not yet the people we know we can become:

I fear to feel Pain
'cause my heart
is not a stone
and bleeds
when touched unkindly.

> *Michael Dupuis*

With the pain that is faced in the pages of the *Carnegie Newsletter* comes anger:

sign on the window
says Learning Front for rent
and you hand me a button
for literacy day and I say
stick it
in your own lapel
while you bury our people
in prisons and psyche wards.

> *— Mike Kramer, on the closing*
> *down of the Learning Front, a*

storefront literacy centre on Main Street, during the international Year of Literacy

With the pain also comes compassion:

Monday I went to the hospital to tutor George Chief, a Carnegie member who was on dialysis; his kidney did not function. I was shocked when they said he had died on Saturday. He was a real nice man. I really liked him; he had so many interesting stories. We had planned to write them. I was really upset when the nurse said he chose to die.

—*Sheila Baxter, author of* No Way To Live

With compassion comes caring, and it is this caring which turns the Carnegie Centre from a collection of isolated individuals into a community:

I came to Carnegie to teach in the Learning Centre, but what has happened is that I have learned so much from so many people who come here. I discovered that friendships go beyond the classroom, and permeate throughout the building.

— *Kathie Leroux*

The *Carnegie Newsletter* is political because it helps people find the power to define who they are, and because of its prophetic sense of justice — the concern with what ought to be. No one is more committed to justice than the editor of the *Carnegie Newsletter*, Paul Taylor. Whether the subject be housing, poverty, unemployment, pollution, or the GST, Paul speaks strongly in defence of the human rights and dignity of the people of the Downtown Eastside.

The *Carnegie Newsletter*, however, is not political in the traditional way followed by many who are committed to political struggle. You won't find many abstract references to socialism or capitalism. You won't find much intellectual discussion about who is left or right of whom. Well, what will you find?

"You don't have to have a degree in English Literature to write for the *Carnegie Newsletter*," states Sheila Baxter in an article commemorating the fourth anniversary of the newsletter. "Just write from the heart about your own experience."

"The values of the heart are dangerous to systems," writes Tora.

Daniel writes with compassion from his experience. "Depending on where we stand, it is sometimes very hard to see ourselves as we really are. If we look behind, we see a trail that is marked by errors. If we look ahead, we can see nothing but distance and uncertainty. It is during these times that we should listen to our hearts."

Pathological liars don't know the difference between a lie & the truth; they mix up fact and fiction. Unlike kids who will fib or tell stories to get attention and sympathy, pathological liars have a form of mental illness.

Fortunately, it's treatable.

JOE PAUL
(1/2/91)

Don't expect to be told what to think by the *Carnegie Newsletter*. "The answer is forthcoming . . . " wrote Garry Gust, a poet and cartoonist. There is a healthy skepticism in the newsletter — "a sense that nothing is what it seems any longer, and that things must be done entirely differently" (Vaclav Havel).

It is refreshing to discover a paper with the passion and sense of justice of the *Carnegie Newsletter*. It is information, entertainment, and inspiration. It is celebration as Thomas Merton described the word — celebration as the craziness of not submitting even though they, the ones who make life impossible, seem to have all the power. It is a joyous expression of the politics of the heart, and it is a fundamental threat to any ideology. The *Carnegie Newsletter* brings hope.

SANDY CAMERON
(1/2/91)

There Is a Miracle

There is a miracle
Which we call a bird of silence
Nobody knows where it comes
    from
Nobody knows where it goes to
But what it brings us is wonderful
And you realize that such a bird of
    silence
Is the most precious gift you have.

VIDEHA
(1/6/91)

Rape Victim

Neither young nor pretty, nor anything in particular, she stood before us on the platform, a single mother you wouldn't look at twice. She'd been shopping for groceries and it was broad daylight. Her arms full of detergent, cans and breakfast cereal, she took a shortcut across a parking lot. The man appeared from behind a car and he didn't carry a weapon, save the one between his legs. He punched her semiconscious, knocking out two teeth, and she told us maybe that was a mercy, because what followed was in the realm of nightmare. She said quietly that she believes her soul left her body, hovering over the two of them as he ripped off her skirt, then ripped into her.

When she got home she burned all her clothes, even her shoes; then she couldn't stop vomiting. Even when there was nothing left in her stomach to bring up, she said, she couldn't stop vomiting. She said she didn't go to the police, because she couldn't bear to tell a man what had happened to her, and the justice system is run mostly by men. She said she wanted to commit suicide, but couldn't, because she has two young daughters. She said she'll be glad to die, however, when the time comes, because she reckons life for women on this earth is not worth living, not when women in every country have to live with fear 24 hours out of 24, and no female is safe, ever, including the one-

(art by Rivka)

month-old baby in her crib, and the 90-year-old woman in the nursing home. She said she thinks about the one little girl in four who is being sexually assaulted by her father or grandfather, and she feels so helpless. She said she thinks about the little eight- and nine-year-old girls in Taiwan who are paraded, naked, in front of sex tourists and businessmen who bid on them, as if they were cattle. She'd read a United Church report that said if these children weep while they are being paraded the men who own them charge a higher price since the male customers prize little girls who cry during sex. She thinks of the women in Africa whose menfolk force them to do all the heavy manual labour while they themselves just sit around, and she thinks of the girl babies in China who are murdered at birth, and she thinks of all the religions in the world that state that only men have souls, while women have none.

Because of all these things, she said, she can't sleep. She feels compelled to check and re-check the windows & doors. She won't go outdoors now unless another woman can walk with her. It's difficult to talk to any man now, she said, without sweat gathering in her palms. In spite of the fact that men are responsible for 98 percent of all sexual assaults, she said, the "decent men" leave it up to women to find a solution. Only Men Against Rape try to work against male violence, and they are a tiny organization struggling for members. There has to be a profound reason for that, she said. That is why she believes there will never be a Royal Commission on Violence Against Women and Children, as feminists have

called for. The insights would be too frightening, and society prefers not to look. Men are unlike other animals, she said, in that the males of other species do not kill their females, whereas the greatest danger facing the human female comes from the human male. For a long time she thought that all women should kill their daughters, then commit suicide, leaving men in sole occupation of the planet. Then they could prey on each other, only this time it would be the strong against the strong. Equality on Planet Earth at last, she said.

In the hushed room, her voice was calm, but distant, and her eyes seemed not really to see us. She had travelled to that country every woman dreads and she had not yet fully returned to us. None in that room knew when we might join her. Not if, but when. One woman in ten is raped, police say, and they are thinking of readjusting that to one woman in eight. In that room were 50 women. That means at least six of us are destined to take her journey. And we lowered our eyes, not looking at each other, and it was obvious what we were all thinking. In every heart beat a very selfish, very frightened, very ashamed and very helpless prayer for survival: "Let me not be one of the six . . . let it be some other woman, but don't let me be one of the six."

DUSTY

(15/5/91)

Reader Speaks Out

A couple of newsletters back Tora wrote that full employment is a capitalist plot. This is wrong. Business is always against full employment because it pushes wages up, so working people make more money and business profits go down. High unemployment drives wages down and makes us poorer. And since people get less money, corporations get more. The poorer you are the less power you have in society and less say in how things are run. This is one of the basic laws of capitalism and capitalists like it that way.

For example, Tora gives the impression that Socred welfare policies promote full employment. Not true. Socred welfare is a system to subsidize low-wage employers, many of whom are Socred supporters. There are different ways that Socreds make it easy for business to pay workers low wages: By keeping GAIN and handicapped payments lower than the poverty line; by paying for privatized employment skills' programs that stream people into low-wage jobs; by paying small businesses that hire people who used to be on GAIN; by forcing people off GAIN into the job market. Even if you pay your employees crappy money, the government will make sure there is a steady supply of people who will take it. They need a high rate of unemployment to do this.

Low wages are the opposite of full employment. A full-employment society promotes high wages and good working conditions. People only work for low wages when there are no alternatives. This is the kind of situation that capitalists and their supporters like Social Credit/Tories/Liberals promote. They don't like full employment because it means that employers have to offer higher wages to attract workers. They also have to offer better working conditions.

When there are lots of jobs, we are able to pick and choose which ones we want. This means that some places are left with a shortage of workers. To get people to fill the job, the employer has to up the wages and provide better working conditions. Because wages are higher and corporate profits slimmer, wealth is spread around a little more equally. Corporations are a little less powerful and the rest of us are a little more powerful.

There are problems with the system of employment and wage slavery that force us to work at making other people rich so that we can make just enough to scrape by. Full employment is one direction out of this because it gives working people more power over the direction of society. As wages go up, working conditions improve and people have more creativity, choice and control in their jobs. For those who choose not to have jobs, benefits like UI & welfare are far better than in high-unemployment societies, like BC. So whether you want to have a job or not, we're all better off with full employment.

JEFF SOMMERS
(1/6/91)

down here

sunshine
on downtown eastside sidewalks
glows fresh crimson
like rose petals fallen
from ransacked gardens of the broken-hearted

from those who wear the violent evenings on faces bruised black & purple
whose teeth are kicked through panicked mouths begging mercy
whose sight is slashed blind by knives of darkness
inside murdered souls whose lives are worn out demolitions
in screaming alleys of vomit & unending misfortunes

& for those crawling drunk & sick
into jaws of rabid doorways & handcuffs of the police

& for those who fall or get pushed or raving leap
from caged-in hotel windows of desperation & hate & grief

& for those lining up more patient than saints
in cold rain & seagull shit to receive crusts of bread

& for those smoking crack beside railroad tracks of uselessness
to derail a birthplace renovated into exile

& for those plunging needles through veins seeking ecstasy
but flowing with nervous shame & misery

& for those whose scared runaway skin is sold
without hope to hypocrisy's ghosts

& for those cheated by political schemes
& are drowned in tidal waves of unknown committees

& for those hardened like steel by the arson
of their childhoods' gentle visionary love of the real
& for the refugees pouring in from the earth's economic wars
& for refugees fleeing wars in the roots of their hair

& for those straight-jacketed into numbers & things
whose withered spirits don't interest
the scientific god who has forsaken them

& for those smelling & looking like death
staggering through whirling neon vertigoes of east hastings
whose leering faces are smeared with rejection

& for those run over by monstrous rush hours of mountains & skyscrapers
of enormous wealth & who get busted for jaywalking a puddle of small debt

& for those whose lungs are wrecked
in a quicksand of malnourished infested tubercular rent

& for those eaten by fears sending them reeling from a breeze turning a corner
or a shadow thrown over them reminding them of all they've tried to forget

& for those whose inarticulate cries for help
are thrown out like garbage arrived from hell

& for those who survive on what's tossed aside into gutters of abundance denied

& for those who have nowhere to be & no way to live
& are somewhere naked & shaking with a life no one else could endure

& for those who are loneliness frozen in tiny rooms & whose mental rainbows of
   aliveness & joy
are sucked dry by fragmenting screens of colour teevees

& for those overdosed on jealousy & bitterness for what might've been
for the bad luck decades that've bitten them & whose frustrations carve
wounds inside & out

& for those whose unshed tears are choking them
or who can't stop crying & die of exposure

& for those who are nothing without a job & have no one to employ them —
except more trouble pushing them out on a limb & over the edge
crushing the life out of anyone beneath them when they fall

& for those fighting terrorizing voices in their heads
reviling betraying & possessing them

& for those who can't help driving everyone else away from them

& for petty sneak thieves stealing pieces of themselves
& for killers of plum trees & the moon

& for the abandoned & damned adolescents
unleashing vandalism & fists of vengeance

& for those whose children are stolen by social cops
& are driven mad by the anguish of unnatural loss

& for those peddling every remnant of innocence
& pawning every friend belonging to them for another fix or a bottle
creating a purpose out of a daily nothingness

& for those who've grown old & left behind a breath at a time
but whose battered dignity is a victory of their own

& for those whose religion is a lottery-bingo-longshot addiction
reversing their history & bringing salvation but whose numbers never get
picked or called & whose horses never come through

& for those struggling to make against all odds an authentic personal change

& for those who can't stand to be alone & can't stand to be known by anyone

& for those picking fights out of a disabled desire for human communion
& end up with their lives & others in ruins

& for those boasting of being on top of
what is obviously pinning them to illusions of mutilated lightning

& for those dreaming plan after plan for escape
but haven't the means to get through yesterday

& for those whose grip on a bottle of rice wine
is at least a perilous future of savage relief

& for those called parasites or pariahs or bums
but who give their last shirt or pass a kind word

& for those whose love is crippled & twisted yet bursting to give
but can find no one able to heal & receive it

& for those picking butts & fighting withdrawal with emergencies
to get through on nothing but stoplights & starlight & "to hell with it all!"

& for those who sentence themselves to die obsessed with bridges & razor
blades & calculations of barbiturates & alcohol

& for those wandering day & night searching curbs & glances for wallets & miracles

& for those fed up & disgusted enough to live quietly out of shopping carts beneath viaducts or hidden in trees in the parks

& for those who've never known a moment's peace & are so dirty & ugly & mean it's worth time in the bucket to shatter self-satisfied expressions of tourists strolling by looking clean

& for those gripped by wheelchairs wobbling on canes lurching between crutches of unremitting pain & whose courage mocks a world speeding by in disdain

& for those deliberately sabotaging every attempt at helping themselves adjust to a mass social madness accurately perceived as more insane than themselves

& for those trying to get by & take care of a family on little more than defiance & love in overwhelmed & worried eyes

& for those collapsing in shadows pissing their lives down the front of their pants

& for those whose tattoos & time dots are the only possessions that haven't been lost or stolen from them

& for those talking only to birds & stones & sweeping evil spirits from the air with magical movements of their hands

& for those longtime lovers & partners holding together amidst years mining down upon them a bad human weather

& for those the most frightening fearing no one & nothing after having fear kicked out of them as soon as they could feel anything

for these my own my selves my tortured prey & degraded predators my sisters & brothers

let my words sing a prayer not a curse to the tragic & sacred mystery of our beautiful suffering eternal worth

BUD OSBORN
(1/7/91)

Silence

Silence is golden so the saying goes,
Silence is also a sign of weakness in some people's eyes,
when all along, they're showing their aggressiveness on you.

Until you discover that silence is your strength,
they will push and pull you, try their damnedest
to bring you down to their level.
Don't let them because silence is strong.

My silence is my weapon.
Everyone envies what I cherish most,
my beliefs, my sense of what's right and wrong.

Someone wants a piece of my silence,
but my silence is not for sale
or given to satisfy someone's greed.
My silence is mine to keep and mine alone.

LARRY LOYIE
(1/10/91)

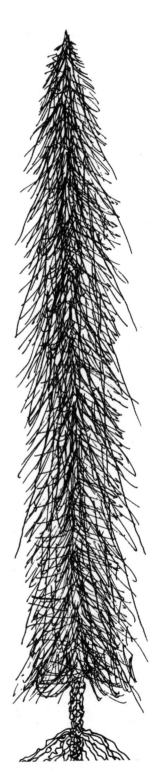

4 DEAR LIFE

1992

From Where I Sit: A Tribute to Danny

There it was on the front page of the
    morning newspaper
        a tribute to one of our community
who had died suddenly and too soon.
Last week the community gathered to
    say farewell
        a moving memorial service in the
    church
a glorious wake in the Carnegie Centre.
There it was on the radio the next
    morning
        a tribute to one bigger than our
    community
the story of how we said good-bye to
    Danny.

I began to wonder how it is that
this 65-year-old Croatian
cookie maker, kitchen organizer
volunteer with seniors
this old country gentleman
with a craggy face
and a warm smile
this loving, sometimes cantankerous
    man
        often single-minded
yet so soft at the core;
could bring together our often-divided
    community
could touch the hearts of those
who never knew him
could be as big a gift in death
as he was in life.

Perhaps it has something to do with
    authentic living
        with giving all that you have

to make the world a little better.

Sometimes people ask me where I find
    God
        in the Downtown Eastside.

JIM ELLIOT
N.D.

the respect no one will give

the respect no one will give
the orange stuck with cloves/a gift from a
neighbour
grudge built that meadow, turned the house into
a pigstie on the highway and pickups nipped up
in the night
took
chickens
and a fat cabbage
and a millstone to grind the sun

MAXINE GADD
(1/6/92)

There's something 2 b said

There's something 2 b said
4 a poem when it takes
a lifetime to write
& 6 seconds 2 b read

ANITA STEVENS
(1/4/92)

A New Season

Oh, time! be slow!
It was a dawn ago
I was a child
Dreaming of being grown;
A noon ago
I was
with children of my own;
and now

It's afternoon
— and late,
boogie and they are grown
and gone.
Time, wait!

GRAM
(1/9/92)

Hello Paul!

Sometimes it's hard to know who are your friends and who are your enemies. I feel that way after reading Tora's diatribe in the May 1 *Newsletter*. He dealt with the March 22 forum called to discuss ways of making life safer for prostitutes, 37 of whom have been murdered. The forum was called because, whether or not you agree with prostitution, it is indefensible to stand by & do nothing while a specific group of people, identifiable by their trade & their gender, are beaten & murdered.

I thought the enemy was rapists, murderers & those who, in their quest for riches, trample on others? I never realized the enemy was me (or Muggs, who has given so much to her community). But why this waste of precious time & energies on infighting. United, we stand; divided, we fall. Isn't our fall what the oppressors & exploiters want? And what do people's social backgrounds matter if they don't exploit others & they're fighting for equal human rights for everyone?! Anyway, if people want to write about me, they should telephone me first & get the facts, not guesswork. To those hesitant to do so, let me assure you I am always polite — unless you make the mistake of trying to redesign me to fit your favourite stereotype. I'm an individual, and I refuse to live in anybody else's pre-packaged, pre-shaped, politically correct pigeonhole. Have a good day!

JANCIS M. ANDREWS
(15/5/92)

Water on Wood

He is reconciled with his three grown children
In the fire-crackling, after-supper hours of life,
  they retrieve these old, worn, fabulous dreams of his
and place them before him. And expect they'll still do.
He stirs to the enchantment the old dreams had always,
his hand recarves the wonder of the old designs,
the loved contours warped, now,
stacked out back, these long ages, out of the ways of people:
  Barely recognizable now.

ABIRTHISTLE
(1/8/92)

Family Viewing: Father

And often he would torture our dog,
    clamping
Tecky's muzzle in his big hand, twisting
till Tecky's head was upside-down
like a black mass, the dog moaning
prayers through its teeth, my sister and
    I
screaming alongside, his other big hand
holding us off, his giggling crackling
around the room, his eyes, coals
under his charcoal hair, our tears
    burning
in his smoking breath.

His fingers were brands
proclaiming ownership
of my breasts, my developing body.
These, and other assaults we never
    forgave.
When he died, only then did we believe
in a merciful God who answered
    prayers.

He never spoke of his childhood.
For us, he was only the Great Fire
consuming his daughters
for twenty-six years. His name
was Tom: synonym
for our hate.

Years after his death, Mother told me
his red-headed father never called him
by name, only "black bastard"
because of his black hair, and that
when Tom was five, Grandfather
    suddenly rose
from the farm table and silently
flung him into the big kitchen fire,
held up the blazer, and up Tom roared.

It took six men
to pull Grandfather off. A miracle
you didn't die, they said
when they pulled Tom out, flesh
    melting
living torch
in his father's auto-da-fe.

And now I know he never left
that place, and that his soul
revolved endlessly about a stake,
finding no way out
through those grown-up faces
and that he never stopped shrieking
his aloneness in those flames,
so he tried to pull
his daughters in.

And now at last I can call you
by your name, oh my Father, and let go
my own burning.
When old hatreds kindle,
I shall stand beside you
in your father's fire, hand in hand,
our flesh unravelling, eyes bubbling
in our heads,
till our streaming tears
put our mutual hell out.

JANCIS M. ANDREWS
(1/6/92)

I *Am* Thinking of Victory

Perhaps it is forever a solipsism, a coin, merely a promise of relevance elsewhere, while around us evolves a tangle of expectancies & connections, the prevaricant rhythms of signature. Perhaps it starts at the peripheries of trivia, working inwards through the glass sunday afternoon of things, through rain & the broad joylessness of stuff, toward whatever it is that lies beneath these patterns of resistance that constitute the thickness of names, our syrupy soup of locality.

Sometime it might happen that, while you are walking along a sidewalk, mostly conscious of the incidentals around you, a sudden panic will arise in the form of a realization presented to you as the following: I am abruptly, convulsively, unequivocally no longer the sum of my past — how did I ever believe that? — but the absence of my past. I am the next second before I decide to do anything.

This must be the opening to freedom. In the same way that we would not speak of imprisonment without assuming peculiar, particular circumstances, so we might do well not to think of freedom without peculiar, particular circumstances. The same applies to just about anything generally spoken of in general terms, like "love" or "politics."

Victory, I think, is existing in that moment of entry, of opening to freedom, the brightness of our eyes there; working always from it.

DAN FEENEY
(15/11/92)

The Tires

coming into the rain, the last cafe
before dark, evening setting like a
   shower
of rust and reckless coffees

tires stacked in a brown slush
by the gate, as silent as dead rivers
that dishearten the freeway

they are small infinities of perfect black
sad mouths of history

glistening brims of emptiness

I stopped driving because of this
excruciating, expected hour, this
unavoidable need for bearings

anywhere, a thin cigarette line
the only comedian

DAN FEENEY
(15/7/92)

in the crystallized processes

in the crystallized processes that made a
   radio around a
pale green blob of glass on a little L of
   brass, in the nimbus of
black holes that laugh at my old man
   and your old man, the
impossible to
comprehend sparkles about the island
   nebulae, the long trip
we have resolved to make to Alpha
   Centauri and beyond, in the
agonized burning of astronauts sent up
   without properly sealing o

rings the plentiful visions of christians
   and buddhists and moslems
and hindus and sikhs and jews

amidst all the procedural wrangling it is
   important to remember
that a southern gentleman can kill
   anything

MAXINE GADD

(1/6/92)

Volunteer Recognition

- **Number of volunteers**   350
- Kitchen labour hours   17246.5
- Volunteer reception
  services   4125.5
- Renovations hours   4831.0
- Learning Centre   8459.0
- Pool room   4279.0
- Newsletter   3028.0
- Patron reception   2073.0
- Artwork/graphics   1285.0
- Cabaret/jams   874.5
- Videos   574.5
- Library   514.5
- Bingo   473.5
- Native cultural   387.5
- Weight room   370.5
- Pottery   286.0

- Ballroom dance   181.0
- Plant care   160.5
- Hair cuts   131.0
- TV repair   86.5
- Special events/
  miscellaneous   224.5
- *Annual volunteer
  hours, total*   *49,591*

The "renovations hours" are what
would have been done if various parts
of the building hadn't been closed off
during. Not bad!

[And this was 11 years ago!!]

PAULR TAYLOR

(15/4/92)

Song 4 Lou

When I saw th coffin my pain broke
     wide open
th man I touched is in that box
I heaved with sobs til I felt I would
     burst
pushed th pain away by gettin rigid &
     angry
so I tell stories mining 4 answers
why'd he do it?
take control with answer make it mine
he didn't believe he was loved
God'll luv ya when U get 2 heaven
there will B no fire escape in Hell
God-Th-Father fire & brimstone
drippin deity on a cross

dry as dust just words in his mouth
why did he create an invisible wall?
& give his power over 2 somethin else?
give his power over 2 an un-gentle
     drum?
slippin & slidin suicidin whap bang he's
     gone
I wish with all my battered defenses
that bits of him were still in my senses
instedda mutilated memories
his voice his face his funny tuff talk
his grey hair & bad teeth & jeans &
     Daytons
he couldn't make it or fake it
saw no future after 40
he packed it in thought he'd never win

it's too late 2 say "don't do it Lou"
U left us holdin th bag
wond'rin was there somethin we coulda
     said
holdin onto each other 4 dear life
4 precious life 4 fragile life

DIANE WOOD

(1/12/92)

Community-supported Farms /
Farm-supported Communities

Did you know Carnegie has a farm? The farm is CEEDS. Carnegie Community Centre Association is a sustaining member of CEEDS. That means people from Carnegie have access to the land, a direct link to your food, your life; something very, very few people have.

There weren't many weeks go by this past year when someone from Carnegie was not helping out here on the farm.

Carnegie & CEEDS have a unique relationship. We are forging a link between town & country by supporting each other. Carnegie supports us in many ways: through the newsletter with articles & pictures, displaying our posters . . . and we really appreciate the interest shown by Carnegie people at our film presentations. Us farmers feel at home whenever we visit Carnegie. The food we've sent down so far has been on a small scale. We should get together & figure out a way for us to send more food to the Carnegie kitchen. It pleases us to know that our good food is reaching the right people. Could the kitchen staff let us know how many pounds of potatoes they go through in a year?!

People ask what security we have living on the commune. When talking about security, maybe we should start with the basics — food, shelter & fuel. Jerry Belanger of Countryside magazine said he felt a lot more secure putting a sack of potatoes in the root cellar than he ever did making a cash deposit in the bank. We know what he means. During our first years at the Borland Meadows,

we'd often talk about the good feeling we'd get when everything on our dinner plate was homegrown. Now we somewhat take it for granted, perhaps not such a good thing.

A lot of our winter's food is now stored in our root cellar — that's our food bank. Our deep freezers are another food bank; they store our meat. We've got free access to firewood. We sometimes use our horses to pull the dry trees out of the bush. We all have adequate shelter & more shelter can be arranged if needed. The basic necessities of sustaining one's life are pretty well taken care of for us. This is a part of our security.

Our animals are part of our security . . . not just for meat, but it gives us an opportunity to live with and share the land with them. This includes the wild animals as well. We need each other; the beaver to control our water, the badger to control the groundhog, the coyote to take care of the gophers. They need us to actively come to their defense. We're beginning to free ourselves from the system, and we're taking our domestic animals with us.

Another part of our security is based on our trust of nature & trust of our comrades in the commune.

We have always maintained that self-sufficient, rural agricultural communes are the alternative to present-day methods of agriculture. The pot-growers in BC have proven that self-sufficiency can be achieved. Twenty-five years ago the only pot available was from Mexico. Then, a number of years later, Colombian came on the scene. When is the last time you've seen any Colombian pot? It's all BC-homegrown now. The slogan "This bud's for you" really has a lot of meaning today. If it can be done for pot, surely it can be done for meat and potatoes.

Well, winter is underway. We have some snow on the ground & as always a lot of things to do yet, such as cutting-firewood and getting the animals in place for the winter season. At the beginning of December we're making a trip to Carnegie with some potatoes, carrots and cabbage. A trip down means a ride back. Anyone interested please get in touch with Bob or Muggs.

COLLECTIVELY WRITTEN AT CEEDS

(1/12/92)

NAFTA

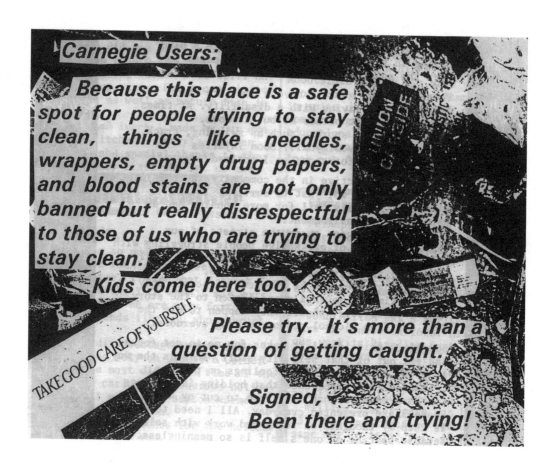

Carnegie Users:

Because this place is a safe spot for people trying to stay clean, things like needles, wrappers, empty drug papers, and blood stains are not only banned but really disrespectful to those of us who are trying to stay clean.

Kids come here too.

TAKE GOOD CARE OF YOURSELF.

Please try. It's more than a question of getting caught.

Signed,
Been there and trying!

To All the People of Carnegie

Why must people always label and judge others on the basis of the colour of their skin, religious beliefs or sexual preferences? The world would be a much better place if we didn't. Each of us is a human being with our own unique qualities that we can share with others. To me it doesn't matter what the colour of your skin is, what religion, if any, you are, or who you choose to have sex with. But what does matter to me is how you treat others.

If I choose to dislike you it isn't for who you are but for what you to do to others around me. I'm writing this on Christmas Eve and in this season of peace on earth and good will to all, remember to treat people with respect and human kindness and maybe the world will be a better place for all.

VICKIE DUTCHER
(15/1/93)

Private Charity Won't End Hunger

People with money will be able to observe Hunger Awareness Week in Vancouver from April 10 to 17. Events will include a gourmet Taste of the Nation benefit dinner with assorted fine wines, including a special private-label Taste of the Nation BC wine; an eight-kilometre run with a pancake breakfast cooked by Taste of the Nation chefs; a gala fashion show; and cooking classes at several Lower Mainland schools.

The purpose is to raise money for food banks, food runners and other private hunger relief agencies. As for poor people, they will observe Hunger Awareness Week by not eating adequately — as usual.

This will be the third year that the American-style Taste of the Nation extravaganza comes to Vancouver. It is no longer simply a well-meaning attempt to solve the problem of hunger in Canada. Behind it lies a view of our society in which our national commitment to a decent standard of living for all our citizens is weakened by the power relations of private charity. The Fraser Institute, a business lobby group, defined those power relations by saying " . . . since it (private charity) is voluntary, it can be cut off if contributors feel it is doing more harm than good" (*On Economics & the Canadian Bishops*, p. 17).

In other words, private charity is a means of control and dominance over low-income people. This view is undemocratic because a decent standard of living is a right in a democratic country. The provincial governments of Canada signed the 1976 International Covenant on Economic, Social and Cultural Rights. This covenant commits our provinces to acknowledging "the right of everyone to an adequate standard of

living for himself and his family, including adequate food, clothing and housing."

The Great Depression of the 1930s clearly demonstrated that private charity cannot cope with public emergencies. In Canada today over one million people rely on food banks & approximately 40 percent of them are children under the age of 18. That is definitely a public emergency, and it brings great shame to our nation.

In a project that spoke directly to the hunger crisis in Canada, a coalition of 28 BC organizations called End Legislated Poverty (ELP) drafted, in 1992, a report called "Waste of a Nation — Poor People Speak out about Charity." In this report poor people allowed that their need for food banks was stronger than the humiliation they felt in having to accept private charity. They did not attack food banks, nor did they ask people to stop donating.

What the people who wrote the report asked for was to end the need for food banks. They challenged people who weren't poor to join them in rejecting American-style social programs where food and housing were provided for the poor at the whim of the rich. They challenged all Canadians to work for a society of full employment and decent incomes where citizens didn't have to depend on leftovers from the tables of the rich in order to survive.

Here are some suggestions that will help Hunger Awareness Week become more authentic: Instead of a gourmet feast for the Taste of the Nation benefit dinner, serve macaroni & cheese, and serve water instead of wine. Have as the main speaker a person from an anti-poverty group that works for social justice. Have a group of people fast for the entire week as a gesture of mourning for our country because it lacks the political will to care adequately for its own citizens. Work with those who are poor to end the need for food banks by reaffirming our commitment to a Canada of full employment, with adequate incomes for those in & out of the paid labour force. Seriously discuss all the ways we can end legislated poverty in our country.

SANDY CAMERON
(15/3/93)

Sadhana

The pain will not set in
It will be revealed as having
always been there —

Thoughts put off — not thought about
    at all;
Just the first line or so
— dismissed as bootless speculation

Yet the universe moves as independent
from wishes/dreams/fantasies
and the feeling is that the Perfect
    Ideology
is biding its time . . . in the shadows . . .
Time to start for home.

Start with the first step and have faith
What else is there in a world gone
    crazy?
With people quite happy to cut out
your tongue and make you eat it.

PAULR TAYLOR
(1/4/93)

heron's long wings beating away toward nightfall

heron's long wings beating away toward nightfall
in the falling darkness the fallen leaves

freighters turning to shadow and lights across grey water
all the way to siwash rock the waves quietly agree

ANDY ALEXANDER
(1/12/93)

To Be Politically Correct at Christmas

I love the sparkles
the reds and the greens
children's contagious expectations
of wonderful things to come
mince pies, turkeys
and cranberry sauce
hugs and greetings
from friends,

Woodward's windows
where crazy bears
bake cookies and pies,
and ducks and mice
skate on ice.
And yet I know
if I didn't have my family
if I were alone in a room
if I had no money for food
if I didn't have money to pay Santa,
if I was a parent
         without present for child,
         if my children had been
apprehended,
         I would hate Christmas
         and surely cry, and probably
         feel suicidal as many people do.

When I was a child I was
         lonely and abused and cried deep
tears
         at Christmas
         as I looked into other families'
windows
         with trees and lights and
         seemingly happy people
         how I wished it were me.

SHEILA BAXTER

(15/11/93)

TAKE
DOWN
YOUR
PANTS

1994

The Real Robbie

The day I met him across the breakfast
    table
sucking his index finger in the usual way
taking stock of me, he got my attention
with a quick flick of porridge to the eye

Then the tantrums,
running all over the house
pulling things off the shelves, dumping
    chairs
to be so beautiful, blond curls, doe-like
    eyes
an 8-year-old autistic terror,
wiping shit on the walls, he stylized
    comment

In time, no one handled him but me
when the anger got too much I'd hold him
'til he broke and cried and sniffled into
    my chest
he became mine and me his and
we fought off the rest

When I'd run away his first response

after they dragged me back
was a punch in the face "how dare you
    leave me?"
big brown eyes finally on my lap
    sucking his finger
content again

So the time went I'd run he'd stay two
    years
it was me and Mr. Shannon on my
    birthday
he crawled over to my bed his was wet
but I didn't mind just traded beds,
brothers do that, you know

Before I left, he surprised us all one day
the years of silence finally came to an end
to think I taught him his first word
running around the house
yelling fuck, fuck, fuck.

R. Loewen
(15/2/94)

Take Down Your Pants

Take down your pants and show us
    your pain While we bask in the after
glow of our sympathy and block all
    your efforts for change.

Take down your pants and tell us how it
    FEELS to be hungry, to be cold, to
be homeless.

Take down your pants and tell us what
    it's like not being able to provide for
your kids

Take down your kids' pants . . . Our
    sympathy will coat you in its
    stickiness, Our sympathy will block
    your throat and stop you from
    speaking about our greed . . .
Our need to make you take down your
    pants and
expose to us the powerlessness we
    create for you.

Take down your pants and do it again
    and pretend for us that this

performance will be the last one
while we prepare you once more for a
harder handful of garbage brought to
you in the form of services for the
poor to improve your technique, to
make you more compliant, to
make you work harder for us for less.

Take down your pants so I can wrap
    you in the old clothes of charity
    while I rub on you the bullshit of my
    sympathy and stop you from
    speaking the truth
or correct your manners.

Take down your pants and let me
    compare you to others I have known
    who were even more in need of my
    demented attention, Those who lived
    far away
and were grateful for my educated
    lasciviousness and charity.

Take down your pants
and learn not to take aim with your
    strong foot in the centre of my
    patriarchy,
my greed, my disgusting need to
    improve but not end the poverty I
    create.

Take down your pants and swallow it.

Take down your pants and in noisy
    compliance teach your children to
swallow it.

TAKE DOWN YOUR PANTS AND
    SHOW US
YOUR PAIN WHILE WE EXPIRE IN
    OUR
MIDDLECLASS POSTURE OF
    SYMPATHY

PATRICIA CHAUNCEY
(15/3/94)

To Janice

You grasped my hand
to touch your cheek
and joked
See it's me
I marvelled at the
softness like my
mother's I thought
Give a kiss to Leith you said
I promise I will
You said you were tired
You were going home to sleep
how profound in retrospect
I know you were tired
tired of seeing your sisters fall
tired of the pain in your heart
Now I understand that pain
because it is in mine
and in everyone you touched
even the clouds wept
and on a beautiful sunny day
we said farewell
how appropriate
that's just like you
everything coordinated
you always had a chair for me
where we held court
keeping the jesters in line

I'll never forget you
standing there in your apron
your smile your laugh your eyes
until we meet again
you do walk in beauty

FROM BRENDA
15/4/94)

Volunteering

Hey man, you don't need to be a college graduate to volunteer at the Carnegie Centre.

While in my fifties I volunteered at Carnegie after coming to the Centre for cheap meals and noticing they needed help in the Learning Centre. I was grateful for the meals since my income didn't leave anything for food after I paid my rent, hydro, phone, and bought needed household items. The New Westminster food bank had a policy that only allowed persons to pick up food on set calendar days and it wasn't working for me. I am at that awkward age between being employable and waiting for my senior pension.

How sweet it is to be able to talk to learners, helping them with their English. "There is no life like it." I wish other retired people, retired teachers in particular, would take on the rewarding task. Not only are there ESL students but there are learners in the drop-in as well. Several long-term tutors have been assisting the staff for years, teaching math, science, and other GED courses.

One of our most qualified tutors is leaving because she cannot get a work permit, and will be sorely missed. Another is planning to go to South America to teach English because they have developed and learned skills tutoring in the Learning Centre.

The Learning Centre is going to have a one-time volunteer dinner, which will come out of the staff's pockets, to honour us! I think this is a great gift from them. I'm sure I can speak for all third-floor volunteers in saying thanks.

DORA SANDERS
(1/5/94)

A Woman Like You

There are times when a woman like you is disguised.
There are many times when a woman like you has moods that question their own celebrated relics.

A woman like you can
be a natural sea on an invisible day or a violent blizzard from an irate heart.

A man like me wonders for a little while and then escapes.

LEIGH DONOHUE
(1/10/94)

Earth

They walk, as if human.
Two eyes, even yet odd;
Uniforms, uni-norms, Unices.
Singular intent myopia.
Propagandists' dream creations'
    superstitions;
Superstitious, irreligious,
Fear bedecked and clothen.
Drop a rumour in the pond of
    frustration,
Watch the ripples.
Leading edge led by the cloth 'round
Choked necks, choked dreams, choked
    beauty.
A mafia of fools decide,
A mafia of religions decree,
A mafia of leper-minds; decaying,
A mafia of ideologues
Paranoid nationalisms, rise and fall,
Rise and fall, again and again.
Only the derelicts and kings remain the
    same.
Poles in a magnetic flux.
'Round flesh of iron.
"Darwin was a usurper."
Monkey trials and another Galileo is
    silenced.
For a while.
Yet knowledge creeps,
On moonbeams.
The controllers know controls.
The Templar Knights of patriarchal
    ignorance
Seed another tragedy.
Divinity is ignored,
Divinity is abhorred,
Divinity is replaced, sterilized, and
    feared.

Divinity is a smiling face.
A mother to a child, to a father's
    sweated brow.
To an open hand, gentle judo.
Divinity is a monkey.
Divinity is the sun and stars as
    openings.
Divinity is joyous music.
Divinity does not need you, yet allows.
The blueprints within, the so-called
Original sin, the sin of origin.
The sin of woman and man to revel in
Each other's divinity,
As if, human.

MARK OAKLEY
(1/8/94)

Carnegie Character Portrait: Al Wilson

At Grey Nuns Hospital in Regina, on June 3rd, 1918, the world saw the birth of Albert Herbert Wilson, better known as Al. His father worked for CNR while his mother looked after six boys and five girls. Al was the seventh born. His first schooling was at Knee Path, Saskatchewan.

"I learned how to do calligraphy at Luxor School in Knee Path. My parents forced us to go to school. We walked in snow up to our knees. Those were brutal winters. The school had two rooms, one teacher, and the students were all ages. The first time I went to a movie I thought the cars in the movie were coming right at me so I'd duck. Back then movies were ten cents and silent."

During the 1920s Al worked on several different farms. He started work at age eight, grooming cattle & horses, stooking hay.

"Three sheaves of hay is one stook and after the binder would tie two stooks together, they'd fall on the ground; you had to lean them together so they wouldn't rot, on a 40-45-degree angle. You never worked alone. People from all different farms worked together." When the Depression hit wheat was 29 cents a bushel. Al was paid five dollars a month to work. He stayed rent-free and spent most of his money on smokes — "Smokes were ten cents a deck; they were little buggers." In '35 Al moved to Saskatoon where he worked for Broadbent's Chesterfield House. He studied at Princess Alexander; his teacher's name was Mr. Trickey. "I saw Gordie Howe play at Saskatoon's

All-Star Game."

Come World War II, Al enlisted with the Air Force in 1941. "I was listed as a fabric worker. Early we used to put fabric on kites, like the Sesna. I went to bombing & gunnery school in Moss Bank, just outside of Moose Jaw, in '42, and then was sent to RCAF Air-Sea Rescue at Sea Island, Vancouver. Sea Island is where Vancouver International Airport now lies." It wasn't until 1944 that Al sailed from Halifax to England aboard the Ville de France.

In Wickathiness, Scotland, Al was listed as a Safety Equipment worker packing parachutes, dingies and anything else needed for survival. He did that work for the rest of the war. "I never saw action in Europe but I did volunteer to go on an airlift to help load equipment. The Canadian boys were happy as hell to get out of Italy."

When Al returned to Canada, he saw his mother in Kenora, Ontario, and was discharged in Winnipeg. "They gave us six weeks to decide whether to stay or go. I decided to live in Flin Flon, Manitoba, working in the mines near Thompson Lake. I was a mucker — just shovelling rock into the mine cars which went to the smelter. The work was extremely treacherous. I saw a few people get hurt down there and I got close to getting killed a couple of times from being too close to the explosions. For breathing we had to use mask respirators — it was very filthy . . . easily one of the foulest jobs ever." Being fed up with mining, Al re-enlisted in the Air Force as LAC, one step before corporal. He left Winnipeg in '53 or '54 and was again stationed at Sea Island. In 1956 he had had it with Air Force life and was discharged. He went from pillar to post throughout Western Canada looking for work, doing different jobs, and wound up in Calgary. In 1971 Al finally settled in Vancouver. "I lived on West Tenth and got by on welfare until 1984, when my pension came. I used to do volunteer work at 411 Dunsmuir. Back then the director was Ruth Armstrong. One day I went for a walk and came across 401 Main and someone doing security said 'Welcome!' That was in 1980 when Jim McDowell was the director."

By 1980 Al had left West Tenth and lived at the Lotus Hotel, then later moved to the Metropole "where they didn't change your sheets for eight months." Al ended up at the Patricia Hotel "where they told us to get out

because of Expo '86. They sent us a letter saying they had to renovate and the day I got it an old man jumped out the window from the fourth floor. We had five or ten days to get out so I went to Glory Rooms. Things haven't changed since Expo."

In the years Al volunteered at Carnegie he became famous for his banners and crazy cards, not to mention the world-famous Bullshit Chart.

"It was an idea I came up with to represent all the people who come & go."

On the main chart there are 15 references and lots of photographs going back to 1980. For 1991 "Muggs replaces Nancy as the #1 sweetheart, and Marty is #2. Nancy will go down as the all-time Sweetheart."

For his volunteer work at Carnegie, Al received commendations from Ald. Libby Davies, Mayor Gordon Campbell, Jean Swanson, Ald. Harry Rankin . . . not to mention all the people at Carnegie.

"Coming to Carnegie is something to do. Without bugging everybody at Carnegie life would be hell. Those Bullshit Charts are all I've got, those and Carnegie."

STEVE ROSE
(1/10/94)

Block the Bridge!

BEWARE
OF
GORDON
CAMPBELL

1995

" We will rise even stronger from the ashes you
say we live in."

"If you have a dream live your dream. But in doing
so don't ask the world to participate in your dream,
without first knowing, that by involving anyone
you may be imposing on their freedom to choose
their own dream."

YUP YUP YUP (whine whine whine)

Someone once said freedom of the press belongs only to those who own one.

The Gastown whine-ohs would like it if the Downtown Eastside had no press. That's why they are trying to silence the *Carnegie Newsletter*. Seems they just don't like what's being reported about them.

Gastown yuppie Lynn Bryson writes in a letter to the mayor (Philip Owen) that she "continues to be appalled" by the content of the *Newsletter*, adding "Why is the City funding this newsletter through the employees of the Carnegie Community Centre? I ask that you have staff review the funding of this group and, if legally possible, redirect the use of those funds which are presently approved to some positive community activities.

"At the least be prepared to remedy the situation at the next funding approval request. In this time of widespread cutbacks it really irks me to think I am paying for this vitriolic nonsense" (letter obtained from City Hall sources).

Well, here's a news flash for the vitriolic Developers 'R Us clique and their yuppie wannabes: Lynn Bryson and the "new gentry" that she represents aren't paying for anything. The city doesn't subsidize the *Newsletter* or its publisher, the Carnegie Association.

In fact, it's the other way around — we subsidize the city.

The Association raises its own money independently. It funds the *Newsletter* entirely from outside sources, and actually subsidizes programs that the city should be paying for — everything from out-trips for volunteers to free chili dinners in five-week months to new equipment for the kitchen, Learning Centre, music program and weight room.

In the last few weeks alone the Association has funded an HIV/AIDS education project, a tutoring project for Spanish-speaking new Canadians, and a community poetry fest.

The *Newsletter* is the most widely read voice for Canada's lowest-income neighbourhood. Because it's financially independent, it can resist political interference of the type Bryson and her cohorts would like to impose.

The Gasbags have millions of dollars of development capital at their disposal; their own propaganda sheet crammed with tourist-trap advertising; and a direct, taxpayer-subsidized pipeline to City Hall in the form of the Gastown Historic Area Planning Committee (GHAPC).

So what's got their knickers in such a twist about this one little voice of opposition? Hearken back to an article in the June 15 *Newsletter*, which laid out some of the background and relationships of the Gastown clique and their financial interest in development.

- Lynn Bryson lives in a $390,000 condo just off Main. In the last year it increased in value, all on its own, by $13,000 — that's more than double what most Downtown Eastsiders have to live on in an entire year. Bryson's an NPA back-room type. She ran Councillor Lynn Kennedy's election

Literacy Day, 1995.

campaign. Kennedy is the wife of architect Gerald Kennedy, who designed the neighbourhood-busting Fort Cordova (8 East Cordova).

• Bryson's brother, Bryce Rositch, is an architect who owns $840,000 worth of real estate in the neighbourhood — his office and his condo. He had his secretary call the *Newsletter* and order a subscription — just to make sure he doesn't miss any hot news. (He paid exactly $16 for this great privilege — the cost of stamps for a year. Perhaps he's waiting 'til Christmas to make a donation.)

• The power-ponytailed Mike (Mr. Condo) McCoy, who earns his living off taxpayer funding of social programs, owns a condo that increased in value by $12,000 last year. He is the sole property owners' representative on the Gastown Heritage Area Planning Committee.

• Jon Ellis and Jim Lehto, two "consultants" (developers' lobbyists) with strong NPA connections. How do you spell conflict of interest? They were appointed by city council to the GHAPC to help guide the future of Gastown, yet they are waist-deep in the proposed Woodward's (Ellis) condomania and the Cambie Hotel (Lehto) conversion to tourist bed-and-breakfast. GHAPC has consistently lobbied on behalf of the rich and powerful and against the interests of the community. It opposed (successfully) the Crab Park pedestrian overpass and (unsuccessfully) the Bridge Women's Housing project — for shame! At their most recent meeting (June 21), they decided they don't want any new social housing projects on their turf. They say any money for social housing should go into fixing up "heritage" hotels that the owners have allowed to run down so badly. Fat chance.

These johnnie-come-latelys have moved into the neighbourhood, and now want to remake it in their own image. Their major social program is to hassle panhandlers. (Just look at the high-security barbed-wire and chain-link compound protecting their BMWs in back of the unit-block of Powell to see what they think of their neighbours.)

You might say the makeup of GHAPC is more than slightly tilted toward those who have an interest in rising property values. There are two property owners, two representatives of business, an architect, a "heritage" rep (Ellis), an engineer and a hotel and restaurant representative. Condo owners are represented on GHAPC by Mike McCoy. There is supposed to be a solitary representative of tenants, but no community group like DERA or Carnegie has ever been consulted on who it should be — not that it would make much difference with a deck so stacked.

These people have no respect for the community. They want everything for themselves, including the papers on our desks.

One thing they won't get is the *Carnegie Newsletter*. It's independent, it's combative — and it's going to stay that way.

RICHIE GURLEWSKI
(15/7/95)

Human Rights Victory

Sharon Kravitz was working at Okanagan Wine Shops Limited on Granville Island. Her supervisor was Kathleen Ross. Ms. Ross made remarks to Sharon and other staff that were derogatory to Aboriginal people and people of other races and ethnic backgrounds. Sharon found these remarks to be offensive and poisonous to the work environment.

In January '93 Ms. Ross told staff to "please watch the Injuns with the sherry." I am sure we're missing several Private Stock. Stand on top of them while they are in the corner."

She also left a note informing staff that: "WE ARE NO LONGER SERVING ANY NATIVES WHATSOEVER, DUE TO THE FACT THAT THEY ARE STEALING (from us & other merchants). DO NOT LET THEM IN THE STORE AT ALL!"

Sharon couldn't take this kind of discrimination and left; she also filed a complaint under the BC Human Rights Act.

On February 22, 1995, Okanagan

Wine Shops Limited, responsible for the actions of their employee(s), got the following order:

- cease all discrimination
- all staff will attend a course on human rights, discrimination & racism in the workplace & such attendance will be mandatory for managers & assistant managers (like Ms. Ross)
- Okanagan Wines has to draft and adopt internal policy on treatment & service of customers
- Okanagan Wines has to put in place a formal system where complaints can be lodged & heard
- Okanagan Wines donates $1,000 to Hey-Way'-Noqu' Healing Circle for Addictions Society

(Well done Sister!)

Bob Sarti
(1/3/95)

THE ARCHEOLOGIST'S REPORT:

WELL, THAT'S IT...
NO NATIVE BURIAL
SITES AROUND HERE.

The BIG LIE!

Too many community services! Too much social housing! If you haven't heard these claims yet, you'll be hearing them soon. Gastown business groups and their friends are out there chanting these words over and over again, telling anyone who will listen that services and social housing are what's wrong in the Downtown Eastside. They claim that there should be fewer services and less subsidized housing for the people living here. They say that would make this a better neighbourhood.

The real problem with that kind of claim is that it's just not true. Over 90 percent of the people living here have very low incomes and use the services. In fact, they get used to the breaking point. And there are thousands of people on the waiting lists for social housing. It doesn't take a rocket scientist to figure out that the neighbourhood requires more community services and a lot more social housing.

So how do people get away with claims that there are too many services and too much housing here? It's an example of the "Big Lie technique." This is a theory of misinformation that goes like this:

The easiest and best way to deceive people is to tell the most outrageous one lie possible as loudly and as often as you can.

The Big Lie is most often used to single out one group of people and scapegoat them. This group then gets blamed for whatever problems are at hand. Attacking community services and housing for people with low incomes is a way to attack the people who use them.

The claim is that people with low incomes are the cause of whatever problems there may be in the Downtown Eastside (here, you can name your favourite problem). The claim is that if there were fewer community services and less low-rent housing located here, there would be fewer people with low incomes living here. The claim is that this would make the Downtown Eastside a better place.

This is an attack on everyone who uses Carnegie Centre and any other community service in the Downtown Eastside. It is an attack not only on anyone who lives in low-rent housing, but anyone who is on a waiting list for it. But it doesn't stand up to the facts.

Let's take a look at those facts. One of the sources often used by those who claim there are too many services in the Downtown Eastside is a list of all the resources available to people who live in this part of town. It has 268 entries. The problem is that a lot of these resources are also available to people in Point Grey, Kerrisdale or even West Vancouver! It's true that Downtown Eastsiders can use the dog pound, the YMCA (if you have the money), or the Vancouver Volunteer Bureau. But so can people all over the city. Most of them aren't even located in the Downtown Eastside.

So if we eliminate all these kinds of services, we end up with a list of 52 (out of an original 268) which are aimed specifically at people in the Downtown Eastside. However, almost half of these are duplicates. For example, DEYAS has a number of different projects, as does the Sally Ann. Union Gospel Mission has three entries, including two for Pilgrim's Market.

If we eliminate all the duplicates, we end up with a list of 26 services for Downtown Eastside residents. Now, these 26 services include two elementary schools, four churches, two residents' associations, and three community centres.

In reality, there are *only 15 services* in and for the Downtown Eastside. That probably compares about equally with just about any other east-side neighbourhood.

The real problem is that this is not just any other neighbourhood. The Downtown Eastside has the lowest average household income of any urban neighbourhood in Canada. People need the services that are here already and could use a few more. It is clear that more services are required and they should be services controlled by and for the people who live here.

People in the Downtown Eastside have worked wonders with what they have. It's never easy, but it's something everyone here should be proud of and fight hard to support. It's important to make sure that property values don't smash community values.

JEFF SOMMERS
(1/2/95)

Beware of Gordon Campbell

Beware of Gordon Campbell in a good mood. ELP met with him and he was nice and polite, saying good things about welfare. Then he let it fall out of his mouth: "People shouldn't have rights. It restricts others, makes it harder to change. You have to be flexible." So if it's your right to get a basic income when in need and this restricts some rich person to get you to work for a starvation wage in any conditions then you are restricting their flexibility and shame on you . . .

"NEIGHBOURHOOD NEWS"
(15/4/95)

Info Insight

It's time to toss you a few positives re: our beleaguered security staff. I believe that some people think that all they do is harass or pick on people. E.g. Have you been drinking? No smoking on this floor! Please take your feet off the benches (seats). Sorry, no transfers. No we don't store things here. No we don't have free food. Do not use our washrooms to shoot up! Don't spit on the floor! No gambling. Three minutes on the phone. Etc.,etc.,etc.

We don't make up the rules and really, they are not tough to comply with. Some people find it impossible to go along with the simple code of conduct we have, and because of that we may ask them to leave.

What you don't hear about is how many times a year we actually save someone's life. For instance, four times in the last year our security found someone in the last stage of life from overdosing. It's a terrible and shocking sight to find someone turning blue as their vital organs stop working. In each case our crew performed life-saving first aid until the ambulance arrived. It would be easy to just wait but our people don't think like that.

A year ago a man was stabbed and was brought into the Centre by an off-duty staff member. His arm was in ribbons and blood was pouring from a loonie-sized puncture wound in his rump. Immediately three or four staff tended to his wounds and probably prevented him from bleeding to death. He was a street person and unknown to us. (He actually returned a few days later to thank us. This is unusual.) Countless times our security women and men have gone far beyond the bounds of their responsibilities to help, like giving mouth-to-mouth to an aged male in the middle of Main St. traffic, who had been hit by a car. (Unfortunately, he later died.)

They've extended the Carnegie boundary to all four corners of Hastings & Main, helping people who have fallen or been beaten. They have been in the middle of these busy streets, directing traffic or breaking up fights.

They don't ask for applause or even thanks; they consider it part of their job and accept the consequences of their actions. What consequence? At present one full-timer is on WCB with a broken hip. Another was punched in the face several times by the companion of an intoxicated female who was being asked to leave. He required stitches. We have been spit on and kicked, stabbed with knives and bottles; several times per day our lives are threatened.

Most threats (thankfully) are not carried out, but when someone says "I'm going to get you (knife you, shoot you)!" it stays with you for more than a day. You are always watching your back (and front).

Many of our staff live in this area and obviously the stress level is extremely high, even after work or on days off.

We don't ask much, but one thing we should have garnered by now is respect for a difficult job well done.

JOHN FERGUSON

(1/3/95)

COMPANY TOWN AND COMPANY PROVINCE

1996

A Short History of the Carnegie Centre in the Downtown Eastside in One Sentence

The history of the Carnegie Centre in the Downtown Eastside includes the rich land that slowly rose out of the sea as the ice from the last ice age melted, the primeval forests of Douglas fir, three hundred feet tall, that stood where the Carnegie Centre stands now, the First Nations people who made this land their home, the settlers who fled the horror of the Old World, the denial of British justice concerning First Nations land claims, the ruthlessness and material success of the Canadian Pacific Railway, the racism against First Nations, Chinese, Japanese, and East Indian peoples, the generosity of Andrew Carnegie, a divided man, and the generosity, also, of the Freemasons who donated the land on which the Carnegie sits, the courage of working people, many of whom lived in the Downtown Eastside, who built strong unions to

balance the power of a company town and a company province, the pain of unemployed men in the Dirty Thirties, the wonder of 18-year-old Willis Shaparla as he stood on the roof of the Carnegie Library during the occupation of 1935 and watched one thousand men march on Hastings Street, singing "Hold the fort for we are coming," the move of Vancouver's main library from Carnegie to Burrard Street in 1957, the museum with its stuffed bear and Egyptian mummy, the Carnegie standing vacant in 1968, and remaining vacant for twelve years, the heroic fight of the Downtown Eastside Residents' Association (DERA) to save Carnegie as a community centre, the gala opening of the Centre on January 20, 1980, the pride of the Downtown Eastside residents who had fought so hard for a living room of their own, the years of turmoil as the Carnegie Community Centre Association (CCCA), the Carnegie Centre, and the Vancouver Social Planning Department worked out a constructive relationship of trust and respect, and the ushering in of a "fresh start" in 1987 that saw financial solvency for the CCCA, major renovations to the building, and the growth of a powerful Carnegie voice through the Carnegie Community Centre Association, the Downtown Eastside poets, and the *Carnegie Newsletter*.

SANDY CAMERON

(15/4/96)

Donald Where's Your Troozers

Aye, an it's bin a loong travel
Synce wi noed yer goode nam.
Ye've payd yer doos twenty-fold
Synce the yere ye fyrst cam.

Wi'll myss thee pipes, thee fiddle & thus,
But moost of all, wi'll myss thee haggis.

It wonders us what path yi'll goe,
And what goode fortyun yi'll come to noe.

Wi'll recool yer nam wyth trezurd pryde;
Goodebie olde frend,

The Doontoon Eesyde

GARRY GUST

(1/11/96)

We're Only Homeless

I wish that I could make you see
that there's another side of me.

I am often frightened, scared and sad
I'm only homeless, I'm not bad.

The world's so big and full of grief
I'm only homeless, I'm not a thief.

People often say "get a job you lazy
jerk"
We're only homeless, and we like to
work.

There is a big misconception, we are not
dumb
We're only homeless, we are not bums.

You think we are dirty and obscene
We're only homeless, and we're clean.

I'd like to plant an education seed
We're only homeless, and we like to
read.

We've seen the world, some of us like to
roam
We're just good honest people without a
home.

We're only homeless.

SARAH HUGHES
(15/11/96)

NEW CITY
OF
FRIENDS

1997

Celebrating Life and Spirit in the Downtown Eastside

I always like to claim the Downtown Eastside as my spiritual home. As a boy I grew up in the shadow of First United at Gore and Hastings. I played soccer in the Sunday School league on the old Powell Street grounds. Many of my boyhood heroes were born and bred near the jungles at the foot of Campbell Avenue. In the early thirties I knew well the damp, soiled smells of the crowded Newspaper Room in the old Carnegie Library.

And now, more than 60 years later, Huddy, my partner, and I, are in Theatre E at 254 East Hastings for a celebration of the life and spirit of the Downtown Eastside. The air is filled with the solemn beat of the drum, prayers to the Creator, the perfume of burning sweetgrass. Citizens of another age tell their stories; artists dance the agonies and ecstasies of their lives and time. We listen to the cries of the poet . . . prayers and curses for the stony-hearted . . . exhortations for the blessedness at the heart of things.

At the beat of the sacred drum, a young voice reads out the names, a roll call of our murdered sisters. For each cluster of names, the lambent flame of a candle quivers in the darkness. With Whitman, Sandburg, and a host of other saints, I have always believed in "a New City of Friends," "the dear love of Comrades." The Celebration in Theatre E, for Huddy and me, was intimation and proof such truths and legends still endure.

SAM RODDAN
(1/2/97)

The Power of Grief

Six years ago I was living across from Oppenheimer Park. On February 14 I heard drumming and saw a group of people holding hands, standing in the rain there. I remembered that there was to be a gathering to commemorate people who had died in the Downtown Eastside. The drumming was soothing and I wanted to join them, but I felt that I might be intruding on something I didn't know anything about. Besides, my baby already had a runny nose.

Soon after, I went to Quebec for a few years. While I was there my friend, Janice Saul, wrote me a letter full of anguish. The mutilated body of her cousin, Cheryl Ann Joe, had been found in a dumpster. She also wrote of two other friends who had been killed. She said that she was "tired, tired of seeing her sisters fall."

Three years ago, on February 14, I went on the march for the women who have died in the Downtown Eastside. There were a lot of people. It was a moving experience, but I didn't really understand it or feel it. Two weeks later my dear friend and so many people's loved one, Janice Saul, suddenly died. I began to understand the power of grief. For those who didn't have the privilege of knowing her, Janice was a Coast Salish woman who worked for many years in the Downtown Eastside; she was here at the Carnegie Centre for seven of those years.

In 1987, Janice began her work at Carnegie at the front desk. She did the job of giving out information and much more. She could intuitively sense what a person needed — be it a place to stay, a job, welfare advocacy, a new pair of shoes or a meal — and she would go out of her way to connect her or him to it. She would report it if any staff person mistreated a patron. Janice had the twinkliest eyes and a deep, guttural laugh. She had an incredible sense of humour which made everyone laugh with her.

She had been involved in unions and stood on picket lines during the 70s. She became the shop steward at Carnegie. She informed her fellow workers of their rights and stood up to management to defend them.

During the summer of 1989 Janice was the supervisor of Oppenheimer Park. There she set up programs for children, teens and seniors, managed a staff of five local students and cleaned up the broken bottles, needles, condoms and other garbage. With her particular style, a mixture of warmth, humour and determination, she told the drinkers, drug dealers, pimps and prostitutes to take their activities elsewhere. That was one of the years that the park was a safe and fun place to be. In the fall, she resumed her position at Carnegie and began to take on more programming

tasks. She organized the children's Hallowe'en, Christmas and Easter parties and helped the teens put on Friday night dances. She believed that busy and valued kids didn't get into as much trouble . . . that prevention was better than rehabilitation. She organized and went on camping trips with the seniors and volunteers. She made everyone feel valuable.

In 1990, Janice decided she wanted to work in the little Carnegie library as well, so she took the training and became the first First Nations employee of the Vancouver Public Library system. When they tried to get her to work at other branches around town she refused, because she wanted to be with "her people."

She then began cooking and supervising on the second floor. She was so proud of the huge, nutritious and creative dinners she and the volunteers served! She bought and distributed many meal tickets out of her own pocket. And that was just her work at Carnegie. She had seven brothers to keep in line. She often fed and clothed them and made sure they were looking after their families and their aging mother. Her son, Warren, is a fine young man.

After work Janice would often go to the bars, supposedly to "unwind," but she was constantly surrounded by people needing material aid, someone to tell their problems to, encouragement or advice. If the police or bouncers abused someone, no matter of what ethnicity, Janice would stand up to them, take their name or badge number, and follow through the next day with a complaint to the police department or licensing commission demanding an investigation. One night we took a young boy back to St. Paul's hospital where he had been hooked up to a machine but had run away because he was being badly treated. They tried to say they wouldn't re-admit him but Janice insisted . . . and she made sure he was well taken care of until he died a few months later.

She would often tell young women to get out of the bars because they were pregnant. And they left. When I was pregnant I would try to drink a draft about once a month. Janice said, "No . . . go home!" and I did. Her orders came from her heart. Janice helped women get victim's compensation when they were beaten or raped.

She was always encouraging women to "get off the streets," to go back to school or to get a job. As a mother herself and a friend to many mothers, she advocated for 24-hour quality childcare so that women could keep their shift-work jobs in places like the fisheries without getting their children apprehended.

I could go on and on. Her accomplishments were innumerable; as an advocate, a counsellor, a human rights activist and a "favourite auntie" to many children, including mine. She was a true friend. I believe Janice was part of the Great Death. She was murdered by all the other murders.

Many people were as confused, bitter and devastated as I was. Her departure left a huge gap in the Downtown Eastside. There was and still is a kind of club of Janice mourners. We're gentle with one another.

During those first days of shock, my Native friends gave me sound advice . . . "Keep a candle burning, smudge your place, don't go out alone, hold onto this stone, release your pain . . . , she wouldn't have wanted you crying all the time . . . let her spirit go." I felt guilty because I couldn't. Elders told me that it would take at least a year to grieve properly.

The first year I was an emotional and spiritual mess. The second year I was moody and melancholy. Lorraine Arrance, another wonderful Downtown Eastside woman whom I knew, died; AIDS took my friend Kenn Mann. But on February 14 last year, as we marched through the streets and I really heard the Elders' words and songs, I felt my spirits lift. After the march I heard myself laughing from deep down inside, like I did before.

In this last year I've been much stronger. I remember our "running jokes." When Janice and I would see a white person acting like a fool, Janice would nudge me and say, "Leith, go tell him he's embarrassing your race." We just used to laugh, but now sometimes I do. When I'm in a tacky situation I ask myself, "What would Janice have done?" I try to reach out more to people in need but I know I will never be as generous as Janice was. I haven't got the energy.

As one very grateful white woman, I thank the Elders and First Nations organizers for allowing me to share in powerful events like this Downtown Eastside Women's March. I truly believe "THEIR SPIRITS LIVE WITHIN US" and strengthen us.

LEITH HARRIS

(1/2/97)

This Is a Letter of Asking

I wish it was a letter of compliment instead to the Carnegie Learning Centre. When I came to Carnegie I had never heard about a volunteer system, ESL or GED, and really wasn't much interested in anything but staying straight with life. I had been terminated from a job in Ontario and had nearly lost my life in a motorcycle accident. I knew I needed a new start but at 47 nobody much wanted let alone needed me. I think I was doing my best not to be a depressed person.

With me being able to learn WordPerfect at my own pace it has allowed me to have another chance to learn to get above a seventh or eighth grade school level; to help others with resumés, cover letters, patients' letters for doctors, clients' letters for lawyers, teachers with examinations and students with essays. It has allowed me to learn to type (business and commerce) and a little something for life. I was thanked for helping someone else to start again. I'm recognized for this and it feels OK. You know, being part of the volunteer staff is a very important place to me and I grow with it most all the time.

I know the vast amount of intelligence that leaves here isn't what the colleges are looking for, not yet, but at the same time there are numerous Learning Centre students who have been allowed to start that new learning process again — the opening up, the new habit of exploring some new avenue of life.

I've observed students get their GED and go on to the next step. These people just didn't have the confidence at the time of the younger, more agile student, or the outlook, but with casual patience, guidance and understanding, they succeeded in their mission.

Please, I wish you could have a look at what I'm saying in relation to the funding. I know it has been a great benefit to a lot of new starters.

Am I allowed to look forward to seeing an act toward the positive on this matter? Nothing in this whole world could make me happier.

MICHAEL McCORMICK

(15/3/97)

Maybe I Won't Come This Way Again

Morning sun is a rare pleasure
which calls me out
to walk west on Pender Street to Clark,
then north to Powell
and west to the fish dock
past the BC Sugar Refinery.
Being Sunday
the Marine View Coffee Shop is closed
but it's closed forever now —
the Port of Vancouver has other plans.
Seagulls swirl and cry in the bright sun
over the Lions Gate Fisheries,
over the Marine View Coffee Shop,
closed forever.
Maybe I won't come this way again.

Fishing boats rock in the slick water.
Miss Amy Polaris New Venture
the goddess, the star, and the journey
are in these names,
and the boats, like Zen temples,
point to the door at the bottom of the
     garden
which opens slowly.
The Lions glisten with new snow,
a small cloud touches Mount Seymour.
the harbour sleeps in golden light.
Where will the boats go when the dock
     is closed?
Maybe I won't come this way again.

The ice plant is already closed, and
it won' re-open — ever.
"Try BC Ice and Cold Storage,"
a sign says brightly.
Under the sign there's a newspaper
     cartoon
on a grimmer note,
a prophecy,
a cry for help,
a picture of some people in a cage
at the zoo.
We know it's a zoo,
the drawing makes that clear,
and in the next cage is a giraffe,
we can see his long neck and small
     head.
Visitors are watching the people in the
     cage,
and a sign on the cage door reads
"Riff Raff."
One of the ice plant workers has drawn
     an arrow
to the caged people,
and written in pencil beneath the
     cartoon,
"After the ice plant closes."
Oh, my brother, my sister,
Maybe I won't come this way again.

SANDY CAMERON
(15/3/97)

He Will Be Remembered

Bruce Eriksen, one of the founders of
the Downtown Eastside Residents'
Association (DERA) and a long-time
member of the Coalition of Progressive
Electors (COPE), died on March 16 after
a year-long fight with cancer. He was 69
years old. Every time we say "DERA"
Eriksen will be remembered, for along
with other residents, he was determined
to build a citizens' organization. Every
time we say "The Downtown Eastside"
Eriksen will be remembered, for he did
much to change the negative image of
our community. "The people who live
here, they call it the Downtown Eastside."

Every time we overcome addiction
and turn to help our neighbour, Eriksen
will be remembered, for that is what he
did. Every time we fight for decent
housing, a decent standard of living
and a decent community, Eriksen will
be remembered.

Every time we figure out what it is we
are willing to die for, Eriksen will be
remembered, for he ignored threats
against his life; if his death could help
the Downtown Eastside, then so be it.
And every time we refuse to quit, Eriksen will be remembered, for Bruce Eriksen never, ever gave up. Every time we
enter the Carnegie Centre, Eriksen will
be remembered, for more than any
other person he fought to win this place
for our community. Every time we find
the courage to begin again, Eriksen will
be remembered, for he was drifter,
sailor, logger, construction worker,
machinist, iron worker, artist, wood-
worker, gardener, social activist, and

city councillor who knew from the
depths of his being what a person who
wasn't born with a silver spoon was up
against in this world.

Under Bruce's leadership, DERA won
many victories in the 1970's including a
bylaw requiring hotels and rooming
houses to have sprinkler systems,
rezoning to protect housing in the
Downtown Eastside, and the establishment of the Carnegie Community Centre.

In 1980 Bruce was elected to city
council as a member of COPE, and was
re-elected for a total of six consecutive
times, retiring in 1993. He was the chair
of the Community Services Committee
and was a tireless spokesperson for the
ordinary citizens of Vancouver.

Bruce came back to the Downtown
Eastside to restore the painting he did
— it now graces the lobby of Bruce
Eriksen Place, fine housing just off the

corner of Main and Hastings [and is shown on page 126]. He also joined with DERA again to condemn the "Friends of DERA" as just too stupid for words.

To Bruce's wife, Libby Davies, and his son, Lief, we offer our hand in solidarity. The challenge he has left us is clear. Now it's up to us.

SANDY CAMERON

(1/4/97)

Lest We Forget

To me a bread line is just as vicious as the line-ups of survivors and wounded I remember during World War II. In wartime we could think of the clean sheets, letters, hot drinks, food, warm smiles from the nurses . . . and much, much more! . . . But what do survivors look forward to today? I have put aside most of my memories of "fighting the Hun" but I cannot forget the nightmares for so many who struggled to survive in the lanes, streets and jungles of our own city during the thirties. Today, with thousands fighting the same desperate battles . . . who cares? Really cares?

SAM RODDAN

(1/4/97)

An Addict's Prayer

Dear Lord, "Yeah. It's me again,"
Seeking Good Orderly Direction
I need Your Higher Power
Just to last another hour,
Without turning to a needle again.
I didn't require help from You,
When chasing one more fix.
I guess for me religion and drugs will never mix
But knowing total abstinence cannot be based on happenstance.
I'm   asking for Your help once again.
Lord, please take this craving,
That for me has been enslaving,
Take it from me now once and for all.
Give me strength somehow,
Please don't let me fall, for I may not pass by this way again.

BONNIE HEBERT

(15/4/97)

A Resident's Notes from Mali

I think the most overwhelming experience I've had so far has been stripping. This is perhaps best understood by comparing Crossroads to the Peace Corps.

The Peace Corps is American. Their volunteers go to developing countries for a period of two years. For the first half of their placement, they learn the local language, integrate themselves into the culture, and seek out or set up development projects on which they continue to work throughout their second year of placement. They receive extensive cultural and language training; they have a well-staffed, well-equipped home base in Barnako; they live in their own houses in small villages of their own choosing; they cook their own food; they have motorcycles and bicycles at their disposal for their own transportation needs. The Peace Corps volunteers I have seen so far are easily identifiable: they are clearly neither tourists nor ambassadors, and yet they make no attempt to hide their Americanness. The ones I have talked to have a sense of purpose verging on arrogance: they are here for a reason and they express no doubts about its validity.

Crossroaders have none of the above. Despite the year of preparation that goes into our voyage, we are essentially parachuted into our situation here. We live, eat and sleep with a host family previously unknown to us. We struggle in the first few weeks to pick up the rudiments of the language as it is spoken around us. If we want to go anywhere, we have to figure out how to get there by public transit (which, I assure you, makes the #14 Hastings look like a clean, orderly affair). We are cautious about wearing blue jeans, sunglasses, hats, running shoes, and about using cameras. We feel guilty if we go to a tourist restaurant or send for something from home.

As I look around at my fellow Crossroaders in these early days, I am struck by a similarity in our appearance: we are all awkward and uncomfortable-looking, like we don't know what to do with ourselves or how to hold our bodies. We all look like the new kid in class at the grade seven dance when nobody danced or talked with you. Perhaps the greatest difference between the Peace Corps and Crossroads is the sense of purpose. They are here to organize communities, to set up local banks, to experiment with alternative agricultural methods, to establish schools, nurseries, centres, libraries, to build dams. We are here on a . . . well, it's kind of a cultural exchange thing. It's kind of hard to explain because most of the time I don't know myself what the hell I'm doing here. We are just here — dependent on the kindness of strangers.

The stripping is the first part of this cultural exchange. We are stripped of comforts, stripped of company, stripped of both belonging and anonymity. Stripped of independence and pride. Stripped of schedules, dietary habits, exercise routines, mobility. Stripped right down to our cores.

The Peace Corps is muscular; Crossroads is skeletal. They dig wells in fields. We dig wells in our souls.

SARAH EVANS

(1/5/97)

Feelings From Behind The Wall

We are here for reasons known only to us. These places never change. Only each of the new faces. Our friends pass. We sit still. Our time will come one day to say "good-bye" for a while, then the question embraces us — "Will I be back?"

We mostly remember our friends, and those of us who are condemned. We have been taken away from society. Some have hope. Others have little or none. To these people my heart goes.

It is here we are put to a test. We must show honour and respect, most of all for others in our situation, or others who call this place home. Each and every person in here has a heart. It does not matter why we are here, we just are. We must make the best of it.

This piece has been written inside of the Burnaby Correction Centre for Women. It is for you the people to understand how it feels to be within the

prison system. Even though we have committed crimes we are still people who care and have feelings.

DEBRA TOUGH
(15/5/97)

The Hon. Allan Rock, Minister of Health

Dear Minister,

Since 1993, 1,222 people in BC have died as a result of drug overdoses. It is the leading cause of death in BC for people who are between the ages of 30 and 44. These figures are staggering and are only the beginning of what has become a health and social emergency in the riding of Vancouver East.

On July 15 community members and social and health care providers came together and organized a number of

actions to draw attention to the grave situation in the Downtown Eastside of Vancouver. This community now has the largest incidence of HIV amongst drug users in the western world. According to a recent BC Ministry of Health study (VIDUS Study), the HIV infection rate of IV drug users is currently 23 percent, and growing at 18-20 percent per year. This means that within two years the HIV rate amongst drug users could be 65 percent — recognized as a saturation point.

Unfortunately, these statistics do not begin to describe the pain, suffering and despair that is part of our community. The community has worked very hard to provide the best possible support and services to IV drug users and to stem the HIV infection rate but the Downtown Eastside is crying out for help. We cannot understand why the federal government appears unmoved to act.

For too long illicit drug use has been treated primarily as a law-and-order and enforcement problem. It seems that elected representatives, especially at the federal level, have not had the courage to look at the real picture and address the social, health, and economic issues related to addiction. Many people in our community have come to the conclusion that more emphasis on enforcement on the drug problem will continue to be a failure in addressing the seriousness of drug addiction.

The community is saying in clear, unequivocal terms that it is critical for the federal government to act; to stop the "killing fields"; to stop people dying on the streets and back alleys from drug overdoses; and to stop the alarming increase in HIV infection.

As you are the Minister of Health, we are looking to you and your government for leadership and help. The National Action Plan on HIV and Injection Drug Use has, in reality, presented no action at all. We need comprehen-

sive health and social harm reduction strategies to help IV drug users. We need the federal government to take a leadership role in providing health and social support, including drug addiction maintenance programs, through a paramedical model.

The 1994 Cain Report on Illicit Narcotic Overdose Deaths in BC provided an excellent explanation of and rationale for what needs to be done. If you or your officials have not read this report, I would urge you to do so. The report is straightforward and clear in its approach, and emphasizes the need to undertake holistic harm-reduction strategies.

I cannot conclude this letter without raising one other very serious issue that contributes significantly to the growing poverty and economic depression of the Downtown Eastside. The lack of safe, affordable and accessible housing is also an area where the federal government should be taking the lead in responsibility. The right to shelter is a fundamental human right, yet there are thousands of people in Vancouver East who live in deplorable, substandard housing or who are homeless. The federal government's abandonment of social housing contributes to growing poverty in the Downtown Eastside.

In conclusion, Mr. Rock, I don't know how familiar you are with the gravity of the situation in Vancouver's Downtown Eastside, or how the community is struggling to survive against huge odds. I would like to invite you to see and discuss our concerns first hand with knowledgeable local people. I know local residents and agencies would welcome the opportunity to meet with you. The Downtown Eastside is a strong and articulate community, but it needs the attention of you and your government to address the growing health and social crisis of HIV/AIDS and IV drug addiction.

Thank you for your attention to these issues. I look forward to hearing from you.

Sincerely,

LIBBY DAVIES, MP,
VANCOUVER EAST
(1/8/97)

the nest

as towers loom
currency's cut
propaganda propagates
addicts od
as cops're loosened
elders're mugged
dealers fatten
children're abused
as eyes're blackened
cockroaches flick
sirens wail
investors speculate
as senses dull
commuters disassociate
politicians squawk
illness inhabits
as bread molds
thieves steal
tourists blanch
stomachs growl
as cameras roll
rumours spread
hotels rot
loneliness aches
as dreams die
traffic grates

The top 358 billionaires are worth the combined income of 45% of the planet's population, the 2.5 billion people on the bottom.

the pious flinch
cries echo
and all
there remains connection
an oasis reaffirming life
something here brings us
together
and unity is our struggle
collective will moves me
where I can't get alone
I am embraced by community
feeling I am home

S MILLAR
(15/8/97)

Editor, *Vancouver Sun*

I am writing to complain about the derogatory language Ian Mulgrew used to describe my neighbourhood in the November 4th issue of your paper. I was immediately offended when I saw the words "skid road" used in the headline of his article. The correct name for the neighbourhood that includes Main & Hastings is the Downtown Eastside. I am insulted by the picture that Mulgrew paints of the "typical" Downtown Eastside resident. I have a job. I pay taxes. I vote. I obey the law. I do volunteer work in my community. I do not have a substance abuse problem (alcohol, cigarettes or drugs). I am not a prostitute. I am not a psychiatric outpatient. I am not a panhandler. I do not have HIV/AIDS/hepatitis/TB. I am not homeless. I have genuinely nice neighbours. I chose to live in this community, in the Downtown Eastside.

Educate your staff. Demonstrate an enlightened editorial policy to match the *Sun*'s new appearance. Erase the moniker "skid road" from the newspaper's vocabulary. Call my neighbourhood the Downtown Eastside.

LISA DAVID
(15/11/97)

Anita at Night

Tall tight angel in a white hood,
Eyes averted, quick, alert and clean.
Nobody knows you . . . Who you are
    . . . Where you've been.
They pull you by your black wing and
    put you out for all your crazy ways,
    night and days.

There's a fallen angel in your corner
    sister of mercy, angel of revenge

You said you saw a jellyfish dancing in
    the cold, black harbour
You said your father was an Aryan
    prince, your mother, a beautiful Jew
    and men were always after you, your
    pack of dogs, prescription drugs and
endless days to run them through.

Surely you saw those amethyst
    windows in the pavement and the
    snake-like
neon signs during your lonely walks at
    night.

Then, you woke up. Your island of fire
    in scorpio and you knew that women
    are warriors too.

Tall tight angel in a white hood. Eyes
    averted. Quick, alert and clean.

Nobody knows you. Who you are.
    Where you've been.

TORA
(15/11/97)

In the Dumpster

binner@vcn.bc.ca
mcbinner@hotmail.com
Fax: 684-8442

Dear fellow binners and binnerettes:
Vancouver isn't the only city to feel the greed of its shitty hall. The mayor of Langley, Scholtens, says there should be no more treatment centres in his district . . . I wonder where he stands on women's shelters. Maybe he is also a member of APEC (the Almost Perfect Economic Conspiracy). Remember Robbie Robertson from The Band: "I just spent sixty days in the jailhouse, for the crime of havin' no dough. Now here I am back out on the street, for the crime of having nowhere to go."

I just read in the *Sun* paper where the powers that be are going to eighty-six the Challenger Relief Map; it's graced the BC Pavilion at the PNE since 1954! The Shitty Barf Board wants to store it 'til March 2000 and then destroy it if no home is found for it. George Challenger spent 252 thousand of his own hard-earned logger's pay building the map

and worked full-time on it before selling it to the thankless, ungrateful PNE. As a child, I was on the tour as a student and as a patron of the PNE. I can still remember my amazement.

This province does not appreciate or deserve any gifts or legacies. To add insult, the ashes of Mr. Challenger are buried under the map. Makes me won-

Love Is What I Need

Love is what I seek
Only love can heal me
Only love can seal my destiny
Only love can shape my future

ELIZABETH THORPE
(1/10/97)

der what will happen to the totem poles once the Barf Board gets tired of them. Hey, here's an idea. Why don't they put a rifle range complete with a Rogue's Gallery in Stanley Park?

Between the lead and car pollution, they could really smile. Woe Canaduh.

But I digress. Help is on the way soon. A Downtown Eastside guru has been appointed — the Unworthy One has many followers; unlike Clark or Mayor McCheese, he has a soul and a brain.

And now a few words to Michael Boulton, if that is your real name. In the last issue you wrote you were born and raised in the Downtown Eastside.

Hey you snotty piece of bug turd: I
(1) don't use drugs
(2) don't defecate in public
(3) don't "mill around with no pur-

pose or direction"
(4) don't "panhandle, steal and participate in illegal activities"!!!

Don't tell me there is no crime, drug sales or prostitution in Shaughnessy or the British Properties. You make me want to puke. If you live here you are an EASTENDER! Why don't you run off a one-way cliff.

End of Story.

PS: Never mind, it's not worth the lost ink.

Remember our own fallen soldiers in the DTES when you buy your poppy.

May The Bins Be With You. And hey, let's be careful out there.

MR. MCBINNER
(15/11/97)

Letter to John Drabble, Editor, *Vancouver Sun*

Dear John,

An endearing beginning, or at least appropriate, given the subject matter of what follows . . .

On November 4 the Lower Mainland section has the headline "Cash infusion into Skid Road fails to stop the bleeding"; prominently pictured is a female addict and, less prominently, a staff person staring at a bottle of rice wine. Immediate reactions amongst community residents/activists/ordinary people were predictably unanimous: outrage.

The author has taken a very narrow view, used the stereotyping common to much of the *Vancouver Sun*'s coverage of our neighbourhood, and warped a plethora of issues into a swan song for the "tried and failed" scenario played

out in the minds of those hoping to decimate Vancouver's oldest community.

Denigration of residents has been an ongoing pastime for those intent on promoting (the one correct point in the article) gentrification. Epithets of "urban wilderness" . . . "locals are an eyesore" . . . "wasted and pathetic scum" . . . "revitalize /clean up/ better people needed to set an example" . . . ring out in the squinted gazes of people now laying claim to their community / their neighbourhood after putting in almost six *months* in the trenches. Condos are playing to buyers as the cutting edge of this wave, and prospective residents are told plainly that conditions on the streets (specifically these disgusting people) will both and all be gone in two,

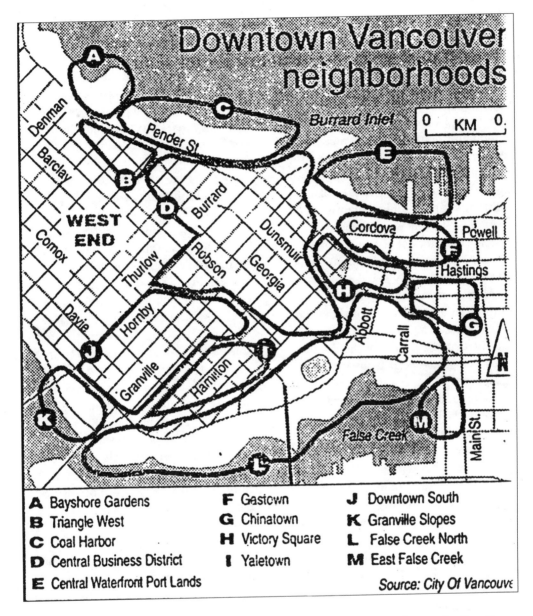

Downtown Vancouver neighborhoods

Burrard Inlet

0 KM 0.

A Bayshore Gardens	**F** Gastown	**J** Downtown South
B Triangle West	**G** Chinatown	**K** Granville Slopes
C Coal Harbor	**H** Victory Square	**L** False Creek North
D Central Business District	**I** Yaletown	**M** East False Creek
E Central Waterfront Port Lands		

Source: City Of Vancouver

three, four . . . years so just sign here . . . Brad Holme, that charming originator of the condo-buyer's favourite exclamation . . . "How can I get my hands on that sorry S.O.B.!?!!" — endeared himself once again to city council, squeezing and squirrelling every concession possible to construct the Van Horne (named, appropriately enough, after the blank

who tried vehemently to privatize Stanley Park around the turn of the century) and its clone across the street at the corners of Cordova and Carrall . . . then had to buy 35 of the unsold units himself (and his mom got stuck with another five units) before disappearing (sorry, re-locating) again to Toronto.

Unfortunately for many of these colonizers, the people of the DOWNTOWN EASTSIDE can't overcome being a major inconvenience to their fantasies. You see, that mythical Valhalla known universally as "somewhere else" is still just a figment of the imagination. All the better people, seeing the futility of showing residents how to be nice poor people, are still using "somewhere else" as a mantra to answer questions pertaining to the disposal of current locals; politicians spinning bureaucratic crud (a synonym for the word used to describe the product of a bull's bowel movement) keep their relation to "somewhere else" relatively secret while talking of property rights and the non-impact of two and a half thousand more condos in a three-block area. This last, incidentally, is part of the double-speak being phased in as the Victory Square "neighbourhood," one of about five neighbourhoods never heard of before in the annals of recorded history.

Okay, the cynicism is getting worn. The difficulties inherent in Ian Mulgrew's piece start with him talking of everything in terms of money. Community centres cost so much, medical aid costs so much, income assistance costs so much, etcetera. It is sad that nowhere else in the Lower Mainland are programs, centres, assistance of any kind evaluated almost exclusively — and in such prominence — as the same in the Downtown Eastside. If the Dunbar Community Centre or (gasp) the West End Community Centre or (gasp in spades) the new Roundhouse thing have programs and services, they are explicitly not shredded on the basis of the dollars spent. Rather, each is evaluated in terms of its clientele, the effort/research/individuals involved in

delivery and numerous other criteria just to get an idea of "what is this thing doing?" Mulgrew, on the other hand, is edited in such a way (if at all) as to give credence to a purely political stance: "This area, this Skid Road, is sucking up money better spent on anything else." And all those who, by default, are among the Best and the Brightest — who have a few thousand/hundred thousand/million/hundred million — can then feel righteous and justified in treating local residents as they would treat a fungus in their Jacuzzi.

The problems of this neighbourhood are real, but not that different from problems in inner cities throughout the world. Money is not being thrown away but it can be better directed into affordable housing, drug and alcohol treatment programs, detoxes, counselling and safe houses for the youth coming here by the hundreds and finding literally nothing but the dregs. Everything we do have here is the result of years of fighting — with landlords, petty bureaucrats, politicians sitting to the far right of Genghis Khan, and the stifling inertia of our beloved society. The Downtown Eastside Residents' Association — DERA — began in 1973 to force landlords to install sprinklers, to rent rooms with doors that closed and windows that opened, to take out the trash now and then . . . Successes, strangely not mentioned in Mulgrew's tirade (not sexy enough?), include the Carnegie Community Centre (the most successful community centre in Canada), the Evelyne Saller Centre, Oppenheimer Park, CRAB Park, the Four Sisters Housing Co-operative (an international model), the Downtown Eastside Youth Activities Society and its Needle Exchange, the

Women's Centre, CrabTree Corner, . . .

Enclosed is a booklet called *Help in the Downtown Eastside* that runs 20 pages and lists just what's been achieved here in the past 25 years. It's just a beginning, but it is the work of a community, a small town in Vancouver. There is little hope that this letter will see print — as just alluded to, it's hardly sexy enough to warrant a place in the new lean mean *Vancouver Sun*. You speak of questioning everything.

Try turning that spotlight on yourself and see how brightly the parts labelled "journalistic integrity" and "fairness" shine out. Here in the Downtown Eastside, questioning the conclusions of unending and dubious analyses is as natural as breathing.

Respectfully submitted,

PAULR TAYLOR, EDITOR,
CARNEGIE NEWSLETTER

(15/11/97)

'A womb is a room without a view.'

READING
THE
STREETS

1998

At Main & Hastings

At Main & Hastings mainly Hastings,
 mainly
getting some air, a place to catch the
 sun
place to watch the moon, the
 mountains . . .

Met Jacob, a ward-mate
from a recent stint in a hospital.
They say if you wait here for 15 minutes
You'll meet someone you know from
 somewhere

Saw an eagle soaring, circling above the
 gulls . . .
Riding high on the Chinatown thermals
It's going to be a lucky day —
Spirit messengers hear my song
All change is temporal, in cycle, like
 Sun & Moon.

TAUM
(1/2/98)

Boycott Conrad Blackism

The so-called newspapers you publish are actually no more than propagandistic comic books, with absolutely no analysis of anything beyond a television mentality view of the world, a corporate, commercial, distorted view of the world, a dangerous and alienating view of the world, so opposite to anything resembling so-called responsible journalism that it epitomizes irresponsible, thoughtlessly automatic, un-investigative journalism, in fact epitomizes all that is mendacious, cynical and anti-human. Your papers whip themselves up into an inane frenzy over so-called fiscal restraint, proclaiming everyday in some pointless, newsless so-called article (really just a fiction, or a remark) that social spending must be cut, because it costs so much (a lie), and there is less money (a bigger lie), while at the same time saying, every day in other so-called articles (fictions) how business, the truly criminal class, considering the history of what the business class has done (as opposed to

Brother, I've 99 chickens and you've one too. Give yours to me and i'll have 100 chickens!

Brother, your want is unfathomable. Please have my chicken!

r. bear

theories about what the business class does, theories which are just fictive lies and wishful thinking, from a class that considers itself so pragmatic but acts in totally unpragmatic and useless ways, for anyone but itself), must be given break after break, tax cut after tax cut, in order to so-called compete (bulldoze) in the so-called world (corporate) so-called market (stock exchange), when in fact all business wants is handouts they don't need in order to achieve goals that will benefit no one, all the while saying that, if they don't get their concessions and cuts and benefits etc. the country will go to hell. The lies your papers spew every day all over this country, which is going to the dogs, as they say, because of its criminal, academic, professional corporate class, not only aid and abet corrupt and cynical politicians and civil servants and professionals and academics in their destructive, unthink-

ing, anti-human endeavors, but actually lead the way, in many ways, toward ridiculous, destructive, thoughtless reactions to just about anything in the world. Your papers act as if, whatever happens in this world, they know it and understand it and thus have some kind of moral or ethical ownership over and above anything that happens in the world, when your papers actually know nothing about anything but what the corporate, criminal, academic class thinks (wishes, dreams) happens, in their insular, self-centered, unimaginative, tired, anti-human old way. Your entertainment sections are just ads for people as talentless, plagiaristic and silly as Andrew Lloyd Webber, the worst so-called composer ever born, whose ineptness at music and sickening so-called lovely, but in fact nauseating, melodies are instruments of torture, examples of music-hating behaviour, not composition (just as your papers are examples of analysis-hating behaviour), and whose popularity in this country is a sign of its pettiness, since the criminal, professional, corporate class managed to beat the life out of everything they couldn't control and to beat the life out of what they do control, destroying hundreds and thousands of creative people in the process, while raising the most amateur, talentless, empty-headed fools to the highest positions, destroying, as your papers do, any opportunity for thought or analysis with a passion that betrays the fear the corporate, academic, managerial, criminal class has of freedom of speech. More than anything your papers exhibit not just a fear of, but a hatred for freedom of speech. Your papers don't even go through the motions of approving of freedom of speech. Your papers have done nothing good for this country, have actually intentionally caused suffering and ignorance and misunderstanding. But you probably don't care about any of this.

DAN FEENEY

(1/4/98)

A Prayer for Children

We pray for children
Who put chocolate fingers everywhere,
Who like to be tickled,
Who stomp in puddles and ruin their
    new pants,
Who sneak Popsicles before supper,
Who erase holes in math workbooks,
Who never can find their shoes.

And we pray for those
Who stare at photographers from
    behind barbed wire
Who can't bounce down the street
in a pair of new sneakers,
Who never "counted potatoes,"
Who are born in places we wouldn't be
    caught dead,
Who never go to the circus,
Who live in an X-rated world.

We pray for children
Who bring us sticky kisses and fistfuls
    of dandelions
Who sleep with the dog and bury
goldfish,
Who hug us in a hurry and forget their
    lunch money,
Who cover themselves with Band-Aids
    and sing off-key,
Who squeeze toothpaste all over the
    sink. Who slurp their soup.

And we pray for those
Who never get dessert,
Who have no safe blanket to drag
    behind them,
Who watch their parents watch them
    die,
Who can't find any bread to steal.
Who don't have rooms to clean up,
Whose pictures aren't on anybody's
    dresser,
Whose monsters are real.

We pray for children
Who spend all their allowance before
    Tuesday,
Who throw tantrums in the grocery

store and pick at their food,
Who like ghost stories, Who shove
    dirty clothes under the bed,
Who never rinse out the tub,
Who get visits from the tooth fairy,
Who don't like to be kissed in front of
    the carpool,
Who squirm in church and scream in
    the phone,
Whose tears we sometimes laugh at,
And whose smiles can make us cry.

And we pray for those
Whose nightmares come in the daytime,
Who will eat anything,
Who have never seen a dentist,
Who aren't spoiled by anybody,
Who go to bed hungry and cry
    themselves to sleep,
Who live and move, but have no being.

We pray for children
Who want to be carried
And for those who must.
For those we never give up on

And for those who don't have a second
    chance.
For those we smother . . .
And for those who will grab the hand of
    anybody kind enough to offer it.

                                    INA HUGHS
                                    (15/4/98)

Listen Up People — It's Tourist Season

That means we're gonna see more GAP-smothered, sensible shoe-wearing, portable camera-holding couples and families on the streets of our Downtown Eastside community.

Obviously members of the Gastown Business Improvement Society have kindly put their time into counselling tourists through their white middle-class guilt after they've visited our neighbourhood and they're damned tired of it. The Gastown business com-munity (or those claiming to speak for everybody) have a new name for the condition plaguing visitors travelling from exotic Chinatown to Gastown along Carrall Street . . . Tourist Trauma. Symptoms include panic, irrational fear of disease, increased heartbeat, unnec-essary perspiration and a strong sense of guilt — all induced by the sight of people with shaggy beards and unkempt clothing sleeping on the benches of Pigeon Park. In one case, a young American woman claimed to have lost one hour of sleep after seeing the sights of Hastings Street. In another case, a visitor convinced himself that he'd caught HIV from seeing a needle wrapper. Symptoms, however, are short-lived and do disappear once tourists enter the consumption zone of Gastown. The Gastown Business Improvement Society's sympathy for traumatized tourists has led them on a crusade of compassion.

In conjunction with the Vancouver City Police, they plan to clean up Carrall Street by adding some vegetation, increasing police presence and creating a Zero-Tolerance Zone for drugs. Since the root of the problem is obviously poor people, the only way to fix it will be through our dispersal. This has already happened in New York, a slightly larger city, where police are cracking down hard on graffiti, public drunkenness and other small signs of the human condition. The result has been a reduction in crimes by poor people through an increase in police brutality.

We must remember that gentrification does not happen by accident, but through the deliberate efforts of capitalistic crusaders who only see good, safe, clean community in rows of nice shops for people to buy, Buy, BUY nice things in. Gentrification only occurs with state backing — the dispersal of the poor through police policy, bylaws and zoning. The police seem to have no memory that, just a short time ago, they pushed the drug scene out of Downtown South and guaranteed it in the Downtown Eastside. All this so Downtown South could be a safer condominium community.

The result of this Carrall Street Corridor is going to be state-sanctioned police brutality. We are setting ourselves up to be a little New York, where the identical efforts have led to such assaults on the marginalized that it's caught the attention of Amnesty International.

Okay Gastown, Chinatown and Police Chief Bruce Chambers — I'll cut you a deal: We won't start our "Mug a Yuppie" campaign if you let us be in charge of tourist protection. I see this as a self-sustaining, for-profit venture, where our employees will charge tourists a small fee for safe passage past Pigeon Park. It's job creation! It's capitalism!! Everyone approves!!!

You could leave us alone. You *could* throw some money at creating a covered, Plexiglas, temperature-controlled walkway leading tourists above Hastings Street. A mural of rich white folks frolicking in the wilderness of downtown Vancouver could be painted on both sides of the walkway so you and they couldn't see the poverty below. Tourists would arrive safe & sound in their consumption mecca and us poor folks would be left to take care of ourselves . . . a win-win scenario.

GA CHING
(1/5/98)

a binner is a true spiritual guide

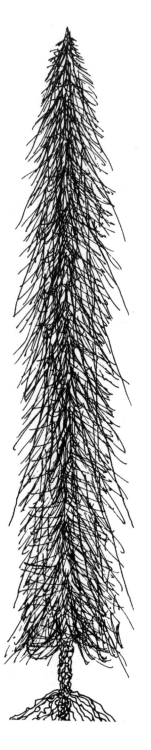
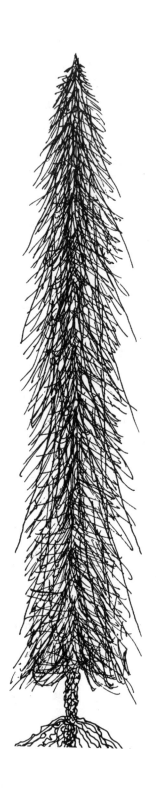

to carl

a binner approaching a bin
anticipates
something valuable
will be found
among the discarded
rejected trash
and useless objects
of our society
a binner is not afraid
to be seen
in deep
and intimate relationship
with what others avoid
like the plague
a binner sees possibility
where others
see the need
for a clean-up campaign
a binner
is a true spiritual guide
let their example
impel
the rest of us
to go
and do likewise

BUD OSBORN
(15/5/98)

A Message from _____

I define my existence as being a prisoner of the planet Earth.

My cell is flesh and blood. Solitary is my confinement.

The sentence is indefinite. Escape is not an option.

For karma's sake I'll do my time until Nature's key frees me.

But only the good are released in youngness, so I'm in for a long stretch of years through endless seasons that rehabilitate my passed-life errors.

The wardens and guards provoke a violent air that spreads through the cell blocks like steam from a kettle.

They praise their Gods but obey their Satans. Their crude propaganda of faulty knowledge is intended to shape the thinking of the inmates who mostly comply like grateful trained whales.

Only in solitary, within the pitch black dungeons, can a prisoner shut out his keeper's brainwashing influences and study the cosmic truths . . .

The cockroach's breathing emits an ancient whisper of spiritual survival.

The wooden plank floor creaks with a song from a long ago forest.

A rat practices comedy on the ledge's stage so my dim eyes will sparkle

applause upon it. Dank, foul air seeps up through ground dirt and sweeps the room with sweet peace . . .

But on the borderline between awake and asleep is where the true light of knowledge flickers for precious moments on Nature's pages, and the prison disappears another day away.

GARRY GUST

(1/6/98)

The Oppenheimer Park Totem Pole

It seems to me
that when someone dies
it is the responsibility
of those of us
who are left
to offer caring
for that life
for that death
in the intensity
of the love that reaches out
from the unendurable loneliness
of our separation.

So did First Nations people,
with their friends and allies,
raise a totem pole
in Oppenheimer Park
on June 6, 1998,
to remember the community
of those who have died
in the Downtown Eastside,
and so did they rededicate themselves
to the struggle
for hope and for justice
from one generation to another.

     SANDY CAMERON
      (15/6/98)

Downtown Eastside Women: Break the Silence Against Violence!!

Women Break the Silence By Speaking Out is a project for women who live or work in the Downtown Eastside to build community, to speak out and to develop strategies against the many aspects of violence that we experience.

This project, which is co-sponsored by Carnegie Centre, the Seniors' Centre, and the Downtown Eastside Women's Centre, will produce a series of workshops by and for the women of this community throughout the summer and fall of 1998. Workshop topics being developed include:

- Violence against First Nations Women
- Violence against Seniors
- Violence against Lesbians
- Violence against Sex-Trade Workers
- Racism as a Form of Violence
- Poverty as a Form of Violence
- Violence against Women With Disabilities
- Violence against Women Who Experience Substance Misuse
- Violence against Young Women

"Women Break the Silence by Speaking Out" will culminate in a three-day retreat for participants. This (hopefully) will be a space where women can take some time out, and also do some long term strategizing about fighting violence against women in the Downtown Eastside.

We are looking for women living in the area, organizers and activists who are interested in participating in this project. We need:

- Volunteers
- Women to work on advisory committees for each workshop
- Experienced facilitators

We are also interested in other workshop topics relating to violence against women in this area that you would like to see or develop. Do you want to be involved? Please call 682-3269 mailbox #831.

STAFF

(15/6/98)

I Went for a Walk

I went for a walk one night because I was bored, but as this time in my life is, so I say, a *lonely* time, the walk, leisurely enough, became something of an *emotional circularity*, and in three hours or so, the time it took me to walk from the house to the middle of Granville Bridge and back, circuitously, I fluctuated between intense happiness, almost giddiness, at some really quite silly things, like the ocean breeze, little good-natured, or whatever the term is, acts or words between people that I happened to witness, to overhear, a lone seagull, a thought about D, and intense sadness, almost depression, at some of the same things, but more at the fatal absence of anything even vaguely resembling community in this city, community based on relationships with land beyond fiscal, commercial, proprietary concerns. The history of so-called progress is the history of land theft, I thought, the conversion of productive, fertile land, by way of very destructive processes, into non-productive, useless *real estate*, and the so-called real estate barons are actually nothing but *thieving and murderous pirates*. It is the easiest, commonest thing in the world to say that dead real estate barons, or dead industrialists, etc., were thieving and murderous pirates. Everyone does it. But no one wants to call the living real estate barons or industrialists thieving and murderous pirates, though they are as thievish and murderous as their predecessors, if not more so. By the time we can be certain of something, I thought, it's far too late, which is why we advocate so strongly, I continued thinking, from our positions of passion, even when we are uncertain of the outcome of our struggles, or whatever the term is, as we generally are. Up and down emotionally I went, not without plateaus, as when I stopped to examine a building or a fountain, to examine some part of someone else's real estate. Everything I know I thought I learned by walking, by looking, by looking at things, by listening, and if I had never ambled, I thought, I would be a complete imbecile. Books are like signs pointing out possible directions to amble, I thought, but the ambling is the thing. We read posters, signs, engravings, graffiti, etc., when we walk, but there is also something very close to reading involved in looking at concrete, fenders, bricks, clothes, trinkets, stairwells, etc., I thought. I'm glad I'm no longer the kind of person to correct someone when they say "eksetra" instead of et cetera, I thought.

If we nip something in the bud, as they say, we are more often than not denying, or destroying, the part of ourselves that can *read the streets and buildings*, as it were, the part of ourselves that learns just by being in a place, the part of ourselves that is *in and of a place*, as opposed to the part that merely observes a place, the part of ourselves that can be involved in something without being *completely defined by that involvement*. Observation of that other, anal-retentive sort, some of us are fond of saying, is willful blindness, or whatever the term is, an example of the same

posture of so-called objectivity that
makes mainstream newspapers so unin-
telligible, so reactionary, so ▨
of and contributor to a world
nipped-in-the-bud thoughts
ings and impressions, the wor
vision and newspapers, and, I
add, the *Internet*. Everything I
proper response or interpretati
according to them, and any oth
response or interpretation is str
There is, we suppose, a way of l
at all these timings similar to am
way of watching TV or reading r
pers or surfing the Internet such
one learns about everything, abou

everything else, by *doing one thing, any
thing observantly, self-observantly but
not over-self-consciously and participat-
ingly*. But the circumstances that obtain
now, we note, almost preclude ambling
or observing, and self-consciousness is
anathema. The world we live in now,
we find ourselves saying, is a world of
people who are either anal-retentive or
who lack any sphincter control whatsoever, a world of strict rules and silly
gestures, of law-enforcers and comedi-
ans, of batons and beach balls.

DAN FEENEY
(1/7/98)

Tirade

we are killing ourselves
in these streets
where I am home
and you are my family
the very ground draws blood
from the foreheads of fallen
    fathers
from the feet of shoeless sisters
and we are killing each other
we are killing ourselves
driven to feed our shame
left exposed in pain
the city shakes our cage
then sits back
watching the mayhem
who we are here
in this ghetto
I am not my drugs

my disease my sores my
smelly clothes dirty skin
my smash 'nd grab
    pursesnatch blowjob foodline
I am a little prince
I am royalty in exile
the kingdom is invaded by
stylish job-fed demons
there can be no peace
no ecstasy rising from
scarred out depths
the day leaves me
disfigured
i've not the spirit to disco

RUPERT B.
(1/8/98)

... That's What Liquor Stores Are For

My name is Margaret. I reside in Vancouver, Canada. I am involved in community issues in the Downtown Eastside and work with the following groups:

- Vancouver Native Health Society — here I am the president of the society
- DERA (Downtown Eastside Residents' Association) — vice-president
- Carnegie Community Centre Association — member of the board and chair of the Community Relations Committee
- D.E. Local 133 — I'm the acting president of this group of community residents who have disabilities
- Aboriginal Friendship Centre Society — member of the board

Most people recognize me as a community activist. I try to help people with issues relating to disabilities, in particular First Nations or Aboriginal persons. This has brought me into contact again and again with the misuse of rice wine in our community. This poison has been killing a lot of our people. It has a very high salt content and is up to 40 percent alcohol. Drinking it leads to loss of control over one's body, breakdown of basic bodily functions, dementia, coma and death.

A majority of people running corner stores and 24-hour stores sell this stuff to make a profit off alcoholics. It is generally kept by the case in the back rooms and is sold for between $1.39 and $6 a bottle, depending on the time of month. Those who work with alcoholics see their "clients" being sold this stuff

every day and are in agreement about this product: it is poison and its sale in this way must be stopped.

The mayor said, on his monthly TV special, that this is a cultural thing! It is not. The Attorney General was asked about it and he gave the same answer as the mayor. More people have died from drinking rice wine than have died from heroin overdoses. People are being crippled and permanently damaged by drinking this stuff and these politicians are hiding behind their spurious "cultural" argument. Their inaction results in disability and death for our people.

The TVs, newspapers and some radio stations have reported on this but seem to sensationalize it with few calls for action. The cost in lives and the quality of life is horrible. Many people who have lost a family member or friend to this poison have stopped me on the street and asked almost without hope what I can do. They feel that I am the only one hearing them.

A few members of the DERA board have met with organizations which represent people selling rice wine or cooking wine. Their demands have been clear — the selling of rice wine and cooking wine will be stopped. The fight will not be over until we do put a stop to it. This community cares about the people who are being abused by the store owners. To us it means stopping people who sell a highly addictive substance to addicts. This needs to STOP immediately.

If you have a personal story to tell

about yourself, or a family member or friend who has lost their life due to this poison, please send it to Margaret care of Carnegie Centre. I am seeking letters of support from individuals and organisations on this crucial issue.

MARGARET PREVOST

(15/8/98)

Trash

We're th white trash, th drunk Indians,
   th niggers, th spics, & half-breeds
We're th ones U call Stupid, Ugly, Lazy,
   Dirty, Good-4-Nothing,
Only Good 4 One Thin
We're th ones with Alcohol brothers
   and sisters
cuz Mom couldn't take it anymore by th
   time she had th little ones

We're th ones who die on dope
cuz it would cost more 2 keep us alive
   with AIDS
We're th ones who get a Shooting
   Gallery
instead of a bed in detox or a shelter or
   a safe place 2 call home
and we don't even get a choice

We're th women who die
because we're sluts, whores, evil, th
   reason 4 all th Sin in th World
that ever was & ever will B . . . howdya
   like them apples?
We're th ones U love . . . 2 hate
We're th ones U love

We're th men who'll die
screaming "FUCK" on th street-corner
& 2 every person we've ever known

We're th ones whose bodies R scarred
   with yr hate
and R hate 4 ourselves

We've had lovers who couldn't make up
   their mind if they loved us
or wanted 2 kill us
We've tried 2 kill ourselves
We've wished we were dead
We've carried hatred like a plague
We've worn R anger as armour

We're th ones who don't get a job
or we're th ones who when we get a job
U tell 2 go back 2 where we came from

We're th children U spanked, punished,
   taught, fondled, touched, abused
molested, locked out, locked in, and
   wished had never bin born
We're th ones U called Stupid, Ugly,
   Lazy, Dirty, Good-4-Nothing
Bcuz we R poor
& Bcuz U were poor
& there's no birthday present U could
   buy us
that would make us forgot R scars

We sang "Freedom's justa'nother word
   4 nothin left 2 lose"
& found R freedom in th buzzed-out
   eternity of drugs
If "th best things in life R free" . . .
   howcum this is th "worst" parta th
   city?

We've watched our neighbourhood get
   worse

We've watched people get paid 4 things
   we would've done
and have bin doing 4 each other,
   anyways

We R dying from an insane RAGE
at having 2 watch people we care 4 die
We have hit th breaking point where we
   decide which memorial
we will go 2 this week Bcuz there R just
   too many
and we don't wanna lose what belief we
   have that . . .
belief that we have in . . .
what?
that there's any reason 2 continue
   praying

that we're still alive cuz of some cosmic
   lottery
or that we're dying of AIDS & ODs as
   punishment 4 th road we took
when all roads lead 2 Main
& if U could help me find that vein,
I could get outta here again
outta my head and th ghosts that haunt
   me
away from that glittering world that
   taunts me
to get more buy more take more
2 feel more like I "should"
instead of how I feel
cuz how I feel is Bad
& I don't like it don't want it
& have spent all my life tryin 2 lose it

somewhere
in some bar
in someone's arms
Close my eyes and make it go away
My family set me on th street 2 float . . .
   like Moses in th rushes
I didn't drown tho I sure have gone
   down

We're born alone and we die alone
and what legacy do we leave behind?
where R th future generations?
and if anybody finds them, could U tell
   me where they're going?
Is my map any kind of map 4 anybody 2
   get anywhere
it's Downtown here . . . or Downtown
   there

& if I could find someone (somewhere)
who doesn't wanna see me beaten or
   broken or on my knees
(and that goes 4 bosses and politicians
   as well as partners)
could we move 2 th Farm
or somewhere where none of this shit
   exists
or will we just stay here
in th here & now
and pick up th shit
& th bones of our loved ones

DIANE WOOD
(15/10/98)

Poverty Pimping in the Downtown Eastside

First we got the CBC coming down here for a live broadcast on welfare day and making a spectacle of all of our lives for the viewing pleasure of the middle class.

Now we have the self-proclaimed **Odd Squad** — Vancouver police constables who are making a name for themselves by videotaping scenes of misery, violence and death that, according to them, are life in the Downtown Eastside. Do any of these men actually live in the neighbourhood? It's more likely that they come here to go to work and then leave for the suburbs . . . or the West Side or even the East Side . . . but not to any hotel room or social housing around here.

How do you think the police would like it if camera crews went into their homes and taped them arguing with their wives, yelling at their kids, having sex, farting, belching, going to the bathroom? And then told us this was all about the police. Of course, that would only be half the story, wouldn't it.

That's just what the Odd Squad is doing to the Downtown Eastside. It's making a video about half of what goes on here. The tragic half. But what about the other half — the solidarity, the beauty that is created by survival and caring? What about people having fun, or relaxing, or doing useful things, like the thousands of hours of volunteering that make this neighbourhood work? You won't see that in these cops' video.

It's pretty easy to find examples of despair and grief in this neighbourhood. We see it all the time. Unlike uptown, or the West Side, or Tsawassen, it's all pretty much out in the open here. Just about everyone reading this will know people who have died from ODs, AIDS, traffic accidents, diabetes, booze, or been injured in assaults or muggings, etc.

What's really important about this place is that in the middle of all that, in spite of it all, maybe even because of it, there is beauty and caring, solidarity, creativity, community. There is not only anger and sadness, there is also happiness and joy.

Finding those things means you have to work at it. You have to get to know people. You have to be their friend, instead of just some guy in uniform. You have to hang around when you aren't at work. And, you have to actually know the neighbourhood and see what's really going on behind the appearances.

So what's the point of the video? Who is it meant for? Is it educational?

It certainly doesn't educate anyone who lives or works in the Downtown Eastside. We live with this.

And how does it count as education by telling everyone else — all the people who don't live down here — the same thing they get told about this neighbourhood over and over and over again? Will it tell them anything about your life? Not too likely. It's just the same old poornography. Since the middle of the 1800s, the middle class has been titillated by accounts, always made by other middle-class people, of the lives of people of the inner city. It's kind of like watching a *National Geographic* TV show. You can be a tourist without ever leaving your living room. It makes life much more comfortable.

The people who write (and now film) these accounts almost always make their reputations by doing it. They become "experts" on the poor, getting prestige and status and jobs for their special knowledge.

Meanwhile, for the people whose lives they've turned into a spectacle, well, life just goes on.

That's what I call poverty pimping.

E.A. BOYD
(1/12/98)

As a Reminder to All and Sundry . . .

Dear Paul,

Thanks for — what can I call it — your very diplomatic note regarding my *Carnegie Newsletter* subscription. I can't believe it has been 12 years — 12 YEARS — since I made a payment for it. Good God. I have received every issue and read them cover to cover. Periodically I pass the newsletter on to other ex-library staffers. I hope you're proud of what you've done with it over the years, PRT — from coverage of political issues to printing real poetry, the newsletter is quality all the way. I always look forward to reading your editorials, and poetry particularly by Bud Osborn and Anita Stevens. I remember Anita from when she used to come into the library and raise hell. She is a genuine artist and would not have a venue were it not for the newsletter. I'm also grateful to hear of those I knew who have passed. There are so many.

This is all I can spare for the time being, but I promise to send in the same amount next year and the next until I have made up for the past 12 years.

I wish you all the best. Keep up the good work.

NANCY
(1/11/98)

Magnum Opus

What is the Magnum Opus? It is not the largest handgun in the world; neither is it a fugue by Tchaikovsky. Magnum Opus is the most important thing in your life . . . that thing around which your life revolves . . . that thing which gives your life focus and meaning.

For me, it was to write.

But today, I seem to be faced with random thoughts.

Or am I like Lewis Thomas writing in *A Late Night's Thoughts on Listening to Mahler's Ninth Symphony*?

Not long ago I was sitting or lying around and suddenly it occurred to me: I hadn't had a drink for almost ten years now — at the end of this year.

Don't get me wrong: when I tell people I did something or didn't do something it is not to make myself feel important. It is to get the point across that if I can do it, you can do it too. Oh, I almost forgot to tell you the most important thing: you might have to get help from Upstairs. I did.

William Faulkner once wrote a book entitled *As I Lay Dying*, for which he received the Nobel Prize. Well, I was about like that, but I didn't get a Nobel Prize.

Or was it like the myth of Pandora's husband? Pandora was given a gift from the gods — a chest containing all the Good and Evil of the world. Pandora's husband found the chest and opened it to find out what was inside and, by the time he got the lid back on, the only thing left was Hope.

Or was it like poor old Harry in "The Snows of Kilimanjaro" by Ernest Hemingway? He'd saved up all of his life experiences, hoping to be ready to write that one great novel, but in the end he didn't get it. I thought that same thing: if only I could get that one great play, that one great novel; after that everything would be all right.

I know now. I'm never going to get that one great play, that one great novel. Do you know why? Because I don't want to.

After all these years and all the things I did, where did I end up? Right back where I started from. And by now I don't want it. To hell with it.

How can I ever explain that? Maybe I can't. I can't put it into words and I'm a writer. Maybe I have found that which is beyond words — the Way, the Tao, the Pathless Path. I don't know . . . and if I did, I couldn't ever tell you.

I do know that I haven't found it necessary to drink anything for the last ten years.

Love, Robert

ROBERT R. RICH
(15/12/98)

ORDINARY
EVERYDAY
EVENTS

1999

In Hope of a Better Past

My phone rings,
A friend is thinking about family lost
. . .
Not by natural disaster,
But by unnatural misunderstanding.
She leads me down the rocky road of my
    own past,
Through doors of resentment and
    loneliness long closed.
Together we pick at mutual scabs of lost
    love
'Til it assaults afresh.
Struggling back to present acceptance
    of past wrongs,
I say: The dead must fight their own
    fights.
We must put away the past
Lest it infect the future.

WILHELMINA MILES
(1/2/99)

My Life is Like the Wind

. . . There is nothing to hold it down.
(RICO, AN 8 YR-OLD STREET KID IN
                RIO DE JANEIRO)

*(This poem dedicated in collective
resistance to the recent changes in the
child pornography law)*

Children abandoned in the streets of the
    world
Their life is like the wind — nothing to
    hold them down
Scattered in sleeping bags
Or huddled together in corners
Sad, hardened faces carved by bad
    weather
Some are dying inside
Displaced, shot on church steps
Pulled out of bed, shamed in school
Made to work 'til sunset
Raped and stolen and assassinated
Slaves to economies
Of prostitution and pornography

Money changing hands
Cold-blooded murder raining
Like the time it got inside and I was
    tryin' to kick it
But it was kickin' me inside

Children kept behind fences
Some making clothing in factories
For the children in North America to
    wear
And some well-dressed children
Drowning themselves
In pools of loneliness and abandonment
Some the bottle and the needle have
    piped
Into the hell of anonymous cars

The children of Ireland
Played in mud puddles and
Underneath clothing lines
Pelting rocks at armoured trucks

And running about boxes of guns
Stored in basements

And some of the children of this racist
    country
Have been reserved contaminated land
And their bodies instead of growing
Like strong reeds in clear water
Were sprayed with pesticides
Damaged by alcohol, stolen language
    and beatings
Children hiding in closets
At seven he hid in cardboard boxes
At 12 pushed to the ground with a gun
    to his head
At thirteen father to an abandoned
    family
Children are hanging upside down on
    monkey bars
Spare the rod and spoil the child

Small adults in baroque paintings
Skipping developmental stages
Collectively we should be calling them
    home
But they've been turned out of their
    father's house

Pawns of the world's power structures
Crushed in the constructs of economic
    pyramids
Last on the list of global priorities

IRENE LAUGHLIN
(15/2/99)

Dear 'Gram'

"Gram" is one of Carnegie's most senior volunteers.

This letter is to tell you officially that the Board of Directors of Carnegie Community Centre Association has selected you as our Volunteer of the Year, and that we are nominating you as our recommendation to be the Volunteer of the Year for the entire city of Vancouver.

"Gram," you have enriched the lives of every person working in, volunteering at or using the Carnegie Centre. I am not going to embarrass you by listing everything you have done for us and how we all feel about you. However, I am enclosing a copy of the letter that the Board has sent to Volunteer Vancouver so you will know how much we appreciate you.

I will say that we all believe that you are a very special person and we are going to do everything we can to convince Volunteer Vancouver to make you the city's Volunteer of the Year. You deserve this and more.

MARGARET PREVOST, PRESIDENT,
CARNEGIE COMMUNITY CENTRE ASSOCIATION
(15/2/99)

Memorial Rock at Crab Park

The Heart Has Its Own Memory
is inscribed on the rock —
Native women lost their lives through
Substance abuse or violence.
Native women: sisters,
    mothers, daughters;
Women close to us.

February 14
We remember
Our people, our women
Abused by the system
Neglected by Native
    leaders.
Too bad here on the
    Eastside
Colonialism rears its head again
Putting native against native — just for
    money.

First Nations traditional people believe
    in the
circle system; others believe in personal
    profit.

For all our relations
we must restore
balance
For all our relations
we must restore
healing
Native Elders, youths,
men, women and
kids,
We are all part of our own
past.

FRED ARRANCE
(15/2/99)

oscar

oscar's dead
oscar from el salvador
sitting there
with a cane
and a black eye
on powell street
said he wanted to talk to me
after the meeting
and though he'd been drinking
sat quietly
until something set him off
and oscar burst forth
with a passionate call to action
a call for us to protest
for jobs
and housing
and decriminalization
and to protest against
the violence of
the police the police the police
and the old white men
aboriginal
latino
ricer
women
excon
afrocanadian
limping bleeding swollen outcast
    junkies
one hundred altogether

cheered oscar
and when he and I sat down
oscar said he just wanted to make sure
the next protest included
the spanish speaking people
of oppenheimer park
I told oscar it was
an honour
for me to know him
a hero
a former combatant
of the farabundo martí national
    liberation front
who fought the salvadoran generals
the land owners
the right wing christians
the cia
and the US corporations
to a standstill
a smile flashed across oscar's face
he pulled up his shirt
to reveal a long thick scar
zippered with stitch marks
oscar said that was where
the soldiers shot him
tears filled his eyes
and spilled down his face
oscar said the soldiers killed his wife
oscar of the inspired speeches and total
    activism
oscar who lived in the mud in the rain
oscar the revolutionary and rice wine
    drinker
oscar who died in the war zone
        of the downtown eastside

                    BUD OSBORN

                    (1/3/99)

While Exploring Self-Same

for Judy Graves

Poetry is like Breathing
sometimes I'm conscious of its presence
sometimes I'm not
It can rise and fall
like a passing thunderstorm
It teases you
with reassuring contradictions
and then leaves you
with your presuming.
Like a dutiful Prufrock
you investigate
life and death in unison:
"Keep breathing!" they say, "keep
    breathing."
We are the lyricists of those colourful
    sunsets
and watch as they lay claim
to the equality of a Burrard Inlet.
Here we are
atop the immortal Georgia Strait
trying to feign spontaneity.
Sometimes the present calls to you
from a familiar place
One that's wrapped with tattered teddy
    bears
and travelling picture ponies.

Is it time to stop?
Rest awhile!
Watch them play with our unruly
    contradictions.
Wonder and imperfection
ticker-tape and cartoons.
Feelings are mixed with reasonable
    perceptions
and then, suddenly, there is only
    thought.
Here a praxis of sorts takes over and we
    leap
into the known like a long lost friend.
I love to steady myself with this first
    person,
or third person . . . it's all the same.
What a cheeky laughter this lad loves to
    portray
I suppose that words and ideas
are competent enough
but sometimes those passengers want
    poetry
to sing colours across all the nations.
"Keep breathing," I say, "keep
    breathing."

LEIGH DONOHUE
(15/3/99)

A Time For Mediation or a Time To Take a Stand?
A Discussion Paper

Solutions to the problems of the Downtown Eastside will not be found through mediation, nor through an expensive office of planners and consultants dropped into the middle of the neighbourhood. Like many of the area's residents and organizations, I cannot greet the Revitalization Plan announced last week with any degree of hope because, in my view, its framework is wrong. It fails to recognize the sociological and historical factors underlying the current situation. It is a reaction to symptoms rather than causes, treating issues of social justice and community survival as if they were quarrels between neighbours.

This initiative seems to be based on a commonly portrayed picture of the Downtown Eastside which misses the mark on several counts:

- The Downtown Eastside is not an empty wasteland that needs new strategies in order to attract investment. It does not fit the pattern of other North American cities where the core has declined because of disinvestment. This is not an inner city that has been abandoned. The problem facing the Downtown Eastside at this time is not that no one wants to invest there, but rather that they do. In this context, revitalization becomes another name for *displacement*.

- The central issue is a land issue. Vancouver's downtown core is a peninsula that cannot expand in any other direction. There are more cranes working in the downtown core than in most other Canadian cities . . . evidence that the central area is still growing. Land in the Downtown Eastside is relatively cheap — cheap, that is, in comparison to the rest of downtown but still out of the reach of the low-income residents for whom this part of the city is home. Many developers are interested in the area. With International Village near completion and the trade and convention centre on the horizon, the pressures for development can only increase.

- The Downtown Eastside is, contrary to popular belief, a stable area. Most of the population consists of long-term residents. Even in the single room occupancy (SRO) hotels, it is not uncommon to find people who have lived in the same hotel room for 15 or more years. It is not a question of instability, but of poverty.

The area is populated by about 10,000 of the city's poorest people and another 5,000 people with low to moderate incomes. In fact, the 1991 census showed that income levels have fallen dramatically in relation to the City of Vancouver as a whole. The widening gap between the poor and Vancouverites with comfortable incomes now means that people in this neighbourhood have incomes at only 34 percent of the city-wide average. This figure is down from 55 percent in 1970.

Many people live in substandard housing . . . in old SRO hotels or rooming houses that have been allowed to decline. (Note that, for this sub-standard housing, they pay some of the highest per-square-foot rates in the city: $350/month for a 10' x 12' room is almost $3 per square foot.) Most of the housing is owned by absentee landlords, i.e. by landlords who do not live in this community. The value of this housing now lies primarily in the land the old buildings occupy rather than in the rental value, so long as the rental market consists of such a low-income population. Renovation is not done except for a conversion to other uses.

The land that the low-income community needs for replacement or upgraded housing is now wanted for development and redevelopment for the condo market. With Vancouver land prices among the highest on the continent it should be no surprise that providing decent housing for the low-income population is no longer a money-making proposition. The instability of the neighbourhood lies not in its population base but in the precariousness of the housing supply for a population whose incomes are inadequate to meet basic needs.

- The social problems of the Downtown Eastside have been compounded by policies of the City of Vancouver and actions of the police in "cleaning up" other neighbourhoods. Several years ago I was in a community meeting with city planners in which an official suggested that the Downtown Eastside should consider opposing the redevelopment of another area (Yaletown) and support the creation of a "zone of tolerance" in that area. Otherwise all the problems of the drug trade and sex trade would end up in the Downtown Eastside. That is exactly what we have seen in recent years: Granville Street, Davie and Mount Pleasant have all gone through "clean-ups" during which the street scene was actually pushed into the Downtown Eastside. Policing standards in the Downtown Eastside were deliberately more lax so that much illicit activity would confine itself to this area. In the summer of '97 there were actually sidewalk sales of drugs out on tables in the 100-block of East Hastings, within two blocks of the central police station.

Meanwhile patrols of both city police and private security were increasing in the adjacent tourist and merchant areas of Gastown and Chinatown. Pressure from the low-income community finally brought neighbourhood policing to the Downtown Eastside, but the situation was already out of control. Drug and sex-trade enforcement and non-enforcement policies have created an escalated street scene that worries residents and business alike, and in which drug users themselves are a very vulnerable and at-risk segment of our community.

the situation we face. Mediation sounds like a commendable notion and is appropriate when there is a conflict based on misunderstanding, fear, or miscommunication. It can also enable relatively equal adversaries to negotiate a compromise beneficial or at least acceptable to both sides. But mediation is not an effective way to protect a vulnerable group against a stronger one, nor to resolve situations of neglect, abuse or violation of rights.

I see the situation in the Downtown Eastside as primarily a land issue compounded by a concentration of Vancouver's social ills. Measures must be taken to ensure the survival of the Downtown Eastside's existing low-income community before this community can negotiate compromises. At this point it would be negotiating away its very right to survival.

MARG GREEN
(15/3/99)

Quotes

'People call me a feminist whenever I express sentiments that differentiate me from a doormat.'

REBECCA WEST

'Whatever women do they must do twice as well as men to be thought half as good. Luckily this is not difficult.'

CHARLOTTE WHITTON

'To recommend thrift to the poor is both grotesque and insulting. It is like advising a man who is starving to eat less.'

OSCAR WILDE
(1/5/99)

C.A.T.

The PPU (Provincial Prostitution Unit) has been functioning as a government initiative for some time, yet has had virtually no impact on the growing trade in kids-for-sex. The prosecution of individuals under Section 212(4) of the Criminal Code is abysmal, with something like under ten charges being laid over a few years and maybe two or three convictions. The law itself needs to be changed, but in the meantime the sky-rocketing pimping of kids is getting covered by individuals and agencies and consultants all looking to get work on both sides. "Travelling roadshow" is apt — with money going to the experts and almost nothing going to prevention and aggressive prosecution.

To get to the point: the idea of establishing Community Action Teams comes from right here in the Downtown East-side, from the group who work with youth at risk directly. Here is where the necessary kinds of services, be they youth detox, counselling, shelter, medical aid, peer safety, bad trick sheets, youth coalitions and on and on, are being provided while people work from this base to get in the face of those with resources and power to make crucial changes. At the same time, the group has been working for a couple of years to create a program that gives people throughout the community knowledge and a procedure to follow when predators are spotted, when kids are being bought. Training workshops, small manuals on suspicious behaviour and what kind of info is needed to proceed with charges and prosecution, what to do with this data and who to contact and what is admissible evidence and how to raise community awareness . . . and it all sounds repetitious after reading about what the PPU is supposedly doing, doesn't it.

PAULR TAYLOR
(15/3/99)

Black Slicker in the Rain

Not just the harbinger of pain
Going to his destination,
Past the junkies to the station.
Maybe he's just sent one in,
Some funky junkie, in a spin.
That's his thing.
Lord of the streets
Checking out all whom he meets.
Black and blue from head to toe
Under buckets full of snow.

Powder.
It rules the streets.
Chews up all that it meets.
Cold and brutal, like the streets.
Seeking shelter from the heat.
From the slicker in the rain,
From the copper, from the sane.

HOLLYWOOD
(1/3/99)

ordinary everyday events

asian male
 said he was lookin for a girl
  to go on vacation with
   the guy paid
    but couldn't cum
     he threatened to shoot the worker
      took his money back

east indian male
 had $100 bill and asked for change
  grabbed the worker
   told her to go with him
    grabbed a knife and said
     they were going to his car
      she screamed
       her brother chased the guy
      away

caucasian male
 driving new red trans am
  picks up working women
   and gives them
    fake $20 bills
     he's very good looking and well
     built

3 males
 2 east indian and 1 caucasian
  driving 4-door blue chevrolet
   pretend to be dates
    and after they pick up a worker
     they ask her for money
      and when she refuses
       these guys pull a gun and rob
      her
       they claim to be from the
      willows gang

caucasian male
 brown eyes
  short brown/blonde hair
   no facial hair

no scars or tattoos
 drives brand new black cherokee
  with black tinted windows
   picked worker up
    asked for blow job
     and after they did the date
      she asked for her money
       he said he already paid
        he threw her out of the car
         and in the process of taking off
          ran over her ankle
           resulting in serious injury
            he also took her shoes and
 jacket

native male
 brown eyes
  short black hair
   freckles on face
    guy was walking
     drunk and edgy
      asked prices for blow job and lay
       said his car was parked nearby
        became physically aggressive
         and tried to grab worker's head
          she retaliated
           with a shot to his head

black male
 drives 2-door red low-riding sports car
  paid for blow job
   this guy was very rough
    held worker by the hair
     forced himself on her

possibly mixed native male
 mid 20s
   drives 2-door purple pontiac
    cruises and stalks women
  sits staring at women
   definitely creepy

caucasian male
shaved head
fu manchu mustache
drives 2-door white van
fishing equipment inside
paid $70 for a blow job
then offered $40 more
if she took off her shirt and pants
he said he'd cum faster
the worker stripped
he went to the front of the van
and returned with a big machete
forced her to bend over
ripped off her panties
and raped her anally
the guy took his money back
told her to get out
and kept her underwear
said he wanted it
for a "souvenir"

3 or 4 east indian males
drive new model sporty looking
  metallic blue car
a working girl hit in the neck
by these guys
with pellets from a sling shot or bb
gun
she says they shot at her
several times

mulatto male
long dark hair
wearing a white shirt and black cap
drives 2-door red sports hatchback
asked for blow job
agreed on date
worker got into the car
the guy began driving
and a second male rose up
from under a sleeping bag in the
backseat
and began strangling her
she'd been unaware

the second guy was there
he choked her so hard
she blacked out
and when she came to
she was lying on a sidewalk
all her money was gone
and her leg was injured
possibly from being
thrown from the car

black male
asked for blow job
without a condom
and assaulted worker
she ended up with a black eye
cut mouth
scratches

east indian male
drives dark blue van
paid for lay
worker started doing the date
the guy was drunk
and couldn't get hard
he wanted his money back
she said no
he grabbed her by the throat
reached behind the seat
pulled out a steel pipe
she managed to get out of the van
and report incident to police

caucasian male
blue eyes
blonde hair
drives blue truck
has history of robbing working
women

FROM BAD DATE SHEETS
COMPILED BY JUDY MCGUIRE
(15/4/99)

Editor,

The "poem" "ordinary everyday events" which was printed in the April 15th newsletter names me as the person who has compiled the reports. They were edited by Bud Osborn into the form of a poem.

While it is true that I type up the DEYAS Bad Date Sheet from which these reports were drawn, I feel the credit should properly go to the women working in the sex trade who experienced and reported these awful events.

It is to the credit of all the women who do this extremely dangerous work that they take the time and care to help warn others about the predators who too often prowl our streets.

JUDY MCGUIRE
(1/5/99)

The Corridors of Death

City Hall — the be all and end all —
Drags its feet, won't toe the line
They pen manifestoes; they put things off
If you make any noise they brush you off
First they etch it in stone, then 3-month delays
Oh, don't bother to phone,
They've got no comment . . . nothing to say.
They'll call your bluff with the runaround
Don't take this guff or let them get you down

We've got the number. We've got the power.
The clock is ticking away, hour upon hour
Put your boots on and get ready to march
To save people's lives and end this Council's farce.

ROBYN LIVINGSTONE
(15/3/99)

Our Carnegie Library Is the Cat's Pajamas

The Carnegie Library, officially known as the Carnegie Reading Room, is Vancouver's oldest library; it was the main city library from 1903 to 1951.

The Carnegie Library contains 10,000 books. About one-third of them are fiction, and westerns are very popular. One-third of them are nonfiction, and that includes history, computer books, biography, and books on health. Another one-third of the Carnegie collection is made up of a fine selection of Chinese books. These books have a high circulation.

The Carnegie Library has an excellent collection of 300 books on First Nations' subjects; it also has books in Spanish and a small Japanese collection. The library contains books that support Carnegie programs, and you will find books on pottery, photography, weightlifting, fitness, cooking, music, chess, gardening and art on the shelves.

It subscribes to 50 magazines and a number of newspapers, including the *Globe and Mail*, the *Province*, the *Vancouver Sun*, the *National Post, Sing Tao, Ming Pao, World Journal*, and the *Christian Science Monitor* (a solid newspaper, not a religious tract). There is a small reference collection at the Carnegie Library. These books can be obtained from the staff by request, but they can't be taken out of the library. The Carnegie Archives contain past issues of the *Carnegie Newsletter*, the *Carnegie Crescent*, the Carnegie scrapbooks, life stories of Downtown Eastsiders on cassettes, history and research, and government publications on the neighbourhood.

Each week articles on the Downtown Eastside, taken from various newspapers, are posted on a bulletin board in the Carnegie Library.

Nothing is wasted at the Carnegie Library. If you have books you don't want, bring them to the library. The ones that don't go on the shelves are given to other people at the book giveaways in front of the Carnegie Centre.

Thanks to all the Carnegie Reading Room staff and patrons for keeping alive the Carnegie Library tradition — books for a democratic society.

DOUBLEDRUM MIKE

(15/5/99)

'we must suffer with them'

we should not look to the bible for
   moral examples
david was a mess
moses was a murderer
and as for christians' vaunted superior
   morality
jacques ellul, a french theologian

and resistance fighter against the nazis
said the second world war
was primarily the fault of christians
because instead of praying and acting
   against it
christians fought for it
and much the same can be said
of christians' response to the war on
   drugs
a real warfare which has arrived
at its current oppressive and
   destructive intensity
from the arrival
of the earliest european christians in
   north america
who called the aboriginal human beings
devils and beasts who were fearsome
   with disease
diseases spread by the christians
   themselves
and the same demonizing language
was invoked in the christian
   temperance crusade
against alcohol
but I wonder how many of us know
why alcohol is legal now
since by any measurement of human
   and social costs
alcohol is the most destructive drug
but when alcohol was made illegal
it created much worse violence
and a new well-organized criminality
and alcohol was never before
so readily available to children
but christians thought prohibition was
   a victory
and now christians promote the
   prohibition
of heroin and cocaine
and drug addicts are demonized

as were first nations people
by the first christians in north america
but the illicit drug war is far more
    diabolical
than alcohol prohibition
because the drug war and its
    consequences
are a global scandal
and the results are everywhere the same
epidemics of hiv/aids
property crime
corruption of police
destruction of communities
and overdose deaths
the illicit drug situation is used now
as a political tool and political weapon
an immensely wealthy and powerful
transnational organized criminal
    enterprise
has developed of such magnitude
that the global economy is now
    dependent
on illegal drug money
and so are local economies like
    vancouver's
but the whole drug pyramid bears
    down
on the lone addict
but mostly addicts who are non-white
    and poor
those superfluous in the new world
    economic order
and in the united states
the drug war has allowed the
    incarceration
of half of an entire generation of young
    black men
and in canada
a similarly apartheid-like percentage of
    natives
are locked up for drug-related offences
illicit drug policies and laws are tailor-
    made

for the booming population control
    industry
but in the downtown eastside

there are numerous storefront christian
    missions
there is the union gospel mission
and first united church
and st. james' anglican church
and st. paul's catholic church
and the salvation army
and a 4square church

and an annual march for jesus
and thousands of young christian
    volunteers
and the results are that
drug addicts in the downtown eastside
have had the western world's highest
    rate
of hiv/aids
and more than 90% have hepatitis c
and while the tuberculosis rate for
    adults in canada
is 9 per 100,000
in the downtown eastside the tb rate is
132 per 100,000
and nearly all of the drug addicts who
live in what has been called
the most wretched and lethal housing
in north america
have backgrounds of severe trauma and
    abuse
much of it inflicted by christians
in residential schools and foster homes
and since the downtown eastside has
    become
fiercely coveted
by unscrupulous upscale development
    conspiracies
wherein christians are directly
    responsible
for the displacement of impoverished
    and
desperately ill people
life expectancy is dropping in the area
an almost unheard-of phenomenon
in a first world nation
but drug overdose deaths
are the leading cause of death
for adults aged 30 to 45
in all of british columbia
and the downtown eastside has become
a slaughterhouse and torture chamber
and what has been the christian
    response

to this preventable genocide
from which they profit so handily?
soup and sandwiches
and flowers for homeless sick
    prostitutes
who are being stalked, disappeared and
    murdered
by serial killers
and hot chocolate for dying addicts
and demoralizing morality speeches
before permitting
malnourished people to eat 2nd and
    3rd-hand food
but christians of course
are essentially concerned with saving
    souls
and to save souls
in a community of poor people
    suffering its passion
a community crucified organ by organ
is nothing less than obscene and anti-
    christ
christian charity is a vinegar sponge
offered to a tortured slowly dying jesus
    christ
jesus was not crucified because he was a
    teacher
or a friend or a healer or a man of peace
crucifixion was a death penalty for
    social rebellion
for those who directly threatened
the religious and political establishment
jesus deliberately broke laws and
    violated taboos
jesus was called a drunkard and a
    glutton who has
a demon inside him
just like a woman I know in the
    downtown eastside
who was told by a good christian
that she has aids because she's a sinner
jesus spoke many more scathing
    parables

about the rich taking land away from
   the poor
and oppressing them
than he spoke about personal morality
but I heard the mayor of vancouver say
"I follow in the footsteps of jesus"
and say it as casually as you or I might
   say
we are going to the corner store for a
   newspaper
but those are mighty bloody footsteps
and in light of the execution on the
   cross
what does it mean for any of us to say
"I follow in the footsteps of jesus"?
and about the downtown eastside the
   mayor says
"we have contained those people
and now we are going to disperse them"
containing the people created
   conditions
of disease and death; dispersing the
   people
will sentence sick afflicted people
to having nowhere to go
no relief for their afflictions
and will spread epidemics
dorothy day who lived both
social justice and the works of mercy
   said

"the mystery of the poor is this —
they are jesus
it is not the decent poor
it is not the decent sinner
who was the recipient of christ's love
but the criminal
the unbalanced
the drunken
the degraded
the perverted
in even the lowest and most depraved
we must see christ
what right has any of us to security
when god's poor are suffering?
while our brothers and sisters suffer
we must suffer with them
I was that drug addict
screaming and tossing in her cell
beating her head against the wall
and not because the man or woman
reminds us of christ
but because of plain and simple and
stupendous fact
he or she is holy"

BUD OSBORN
(1/4/99)

100-Block

A couple was hit by a car today right in the middle of the 100-block East Hastings by a westbound vehicle. Someone told me that both were killed. Angus, John and I walked over to Hastings from Cordova where we got off a bus at 5 pm. I carried Angus, who's four, while coaxing a tired, complaining John, who's six, to see why Hastings Street was blocked off. Traffic was diverted throughout rush hour.

"Killed at 3 o'clock," a young native woman who stood watching with her mother and son said. "They took the man away half an hour ago. The woman lived but died on the way to the hospital." I wondered how she'd know so much. Perhaps it will be in the papers. (I later heard it on CBC as a traffic report.)

My friend and I joke about the 100 block — ground zero — the core of our most impoverished neighbourhood. If the world comes to an end it ends here first. Scores of people brave the heavy traffic of Hastings Street to go from the Balmoral to the Regent, from the Brandiz to the Sunrise to score drugs or to socialize. We wonder if someone could paint a couple of crosswalks diagonally mid-block like the hippies did on Fourth Avenue in 1970 . . . from the Last Chance Saloon to the Golden Palace Opera House because Fourth Avenue became a steady stream of cars coming to gawk at the hippies. What self-respecting outlaw low-life would walk to the corner to cross, obedient to the machine? Crossing against the light and jaywalking are acts of defiance. Vancouver's most oppressed, never-to-be-employed, soon-to-be-dead citizens can still courageously muster (even loaded or hung-over) a "fuck you" to motorists — suburban commuters — all "haves" in this "have-not" neighbourhood. The inconvenience of hitting someone could ruin their whole day.

Sometimes I stand on Hastings Street and observe the change since the 1970s. I remember there were folks, regular people, some with jobs, some without, who were old, young, shopping, drunk, walking by, transferring buses, and in the background when I trained my eye and watched long enough I could spot nervous addicts scoring drugs from skulking dealers. Now it takes time to spot people with jobs from boosters, addicts and drugged mental health consumers who crowd the wide sidewalks.

A small white City Works truck was parked in front of the Washington Hotel near a large white piece of paper on the road. The city workers get out and lift up the paper while a fireman stands at the ready, a hose in his hands. There are guts — internal organs of the squashed pedestrian — left on the road surrounded by a wide stain of blood. I'm horrified that they can't pick them up and dispose of them in a more dignified way. I wondered which organs they were . . . what falls out of us when we are split open, whacked by a car.

Ground zero was quiet; for once peaceful with no cars, buses and trucks thundering by. A pear is squashed flat closer to the curb in front of us and a clear plastic cup and spoon lay on the pavement. Was this their last meal? If

we stood quietly could we feel their spirits lingering nearby, shocked by sudden violent death?

As I stood holding my four-year-old, I turned his head into my shoulder away from the guts dancing along the asphalt, chased by the water from the firehose. John stared transfixed. I reached out and firmly pulled him to me, hugging him to my legs, my arm across his heart from behind and moaned a long low grieving noise. Tears welled in my eyes. "Let's go home now."

Spit and gum litter the wide sidewalk and the stench of urine concentrated by a rare long spell of no rain wafts from a nearby alley, causing the kids to plug their noses. A man drunk/passed out against a boarded-up storefront stirs as we walk slowly by. Dealers and sick addicts are selling, complaining and scheming in small groups across the street by the Carnegie Centre and the Roosevelt Hotel, oblivious to the sombreness that has settled on their clean, dry neighbours and the two dozen or so cops and firemen loitering at the death scene.

I want to know who died. My boys worry it might be our friend who drinks too much — that he might have staggered onto the road. I sense whoever died had more spent on this untidy death scene than on their uncelebrated lives. I know the coroner won't tell who died as they will only confirm the death of someone you name.

I feel angry and suppress an urge to shout at the cold just-doing-their-job firefighters and cops and at passersby, spectators. I have to know who else cares and I'm embarrassed that I cried. I wonder how my children will understand that the inconvenience of this traffic diversion and mess on the road mean more than some people's lives. But I really wonder if those bloody human guts dancing along the gutter will slip through the grate of the storm sewer.

ANN LIVINGSTON

(15/5/99)

More of the Same

The Haven, an overnight shelter for homeless men, was set up for a six-month trial to see if it would "work." It has. The Salvation Army has made an application to the city to have whatever needs to be changed changed so The Haven is a permanent facility. The City asked for community input and, lo and behold, the Gastown nitwits are crying about all the terrible things such a facility will do to them and theirs.

The Gastown Historic Area Planning Committee is appointed by city council; there were six people at a meeting and, in a 4-2 vote, they passed a motion to condemn the Sally Ann's proposal. This is the kind of sick situation that other community stuff gets mired in — four people in Gastown claiming some kind of superiority use an old-boy vested-interest connection (being appointed by the very people who now approve or deny this proposal) to condemn or attack things that are obviously needed in our community and do so as if they have more say or sway than elected representatives or community workers in determining what is really needed and wanted in the Downtown Eastside.

Examples: Pulling bureaucratic strings to kill a probation facility near Pigeon Park; condemning Bridge Housing Society's plan to build decent premises for battered women and a new home for the Downtown Eastside Women's Centre on the lot across from the Columbia Hotel . . . and then working-under-the-rock to tie it up in court for almost three years with some lunacy about a friendly-to-them architect having some technical (*divine*?) right to

build whatever goes on that piece of land no matter who's paying the tab! They slipped with the Carrall Street corridor — meetings began with interested people and reps from several groups like Carnegie and DERA, and the handful of Gastown grunge passing themselves off as "reps" of Homeowners & Residents & Historic Planners & Safety Society & Business Improvement & Merchants & Land Use & the Venerable Clique of Hot Dog Handlers . . . and as soon as our issues of poverty and homelessness and treatment and detoxes and community needs were on the table the "reps" pull off the gloves and write open letters and hold press conferences saying that we have no right to live here anymore. The more idiotic among them have called home-lessness a lifestyle choice. The more stoned among them have decried any resource centre or treatment of addiction and related illness as unacceptable in their backyard.

Is all this a coincidence? How coincidental is it when heroin use is rampant among teenagers and parents find out that treatment or programs are being cut back or even eliminated while hundreds of thousands of dollars go to street surveillance and millions to more cops because it gets political brownie points? How coincidental is it when jails are full to bursting and cops arrest dealers and muggers and they're back on the street before the same cop finishes the paperwork — and addiction grows and efforts at harm reduction, dealing with homelessness and addiction as health issues and poverty as violence against children are condemned by narrow-minded, greedy, classist twerps as unacceptable in their backyard?

This began as news about The Haven. If the Salvation Army's request for permanent status is denied, expect more bars on windows and locks on doors, surely, but more sadly expect more and younger addicts and homeless people on the streets. Think about the mindsets of the Gastown blanks when thinking about kids killing other kids in schools and in gangs. When hope is dashed, when drugs flood communities and treatment is unavailable, killing something makes sense.

Paul R Taylor
(1/6/99)

Shit Saves Us

It's a bad time to be falling in love
because it's not going to last
People want their own way *so* much
They are willing to sacrifice their lovers
And expectations, about getting our
    own way,
are so high; there is no compromise
I loved, and was beaten to shit.

It's a bad time to be writing poetry
Because no one listens to it, excepting
    the Poets
Poetry books have to be glossy and
    glamorous
These books are so cheap that they can't
    save
the poets who write them
People seem willing to sacrifice their
    solitude
For an hour of adventure
There is no compromise
I wrote poetry, and was beaten to shit

It's a difficult time to have friends
because it's not going to last
People want their own doctrine so much
They are willing to sacrifice their
    friendships
And Expectations, about getting their
    own things,
are so high, there is no compromise
I befriended, and was beaten to shit.

It's a good time to eat shit
Because everyone wants to give it
And nobody will take it anymore
We despise any form of constructive
    criticism
And *destructive* criticism is anathema
So there is no compromise
I took shit and gave it and have
    concluded
There is no time like the present, to eat
    shit

We can now learn shit about shit
So take the opportunity; it may not last
For the 20th Century is drawing to a
    close
People won't take shit, and there's no
    compromise,
And no time like the present, for shit
    save us

How can shit save us?
We cannot keep washing it into the sea
    so
Analyze it, try it, mix it with mother
    earth,
use it as fertilizer
manage it, make it last
For fish are frying, and humans will be
    next
Take this solution to the Old Ones
Perhaps they know a Way
Because, as you and you say, I know
    shit

RUDOLF PENNER
(15/6/99)

The Song of Joan

My name is Anita Stevens. I've been resident in the community for 13 years. I consider myself honoured and privileged to live in the Downtown East side. I was honoured again two days ago when Father John David Retter of St. James' Anglican Church telephoned me to say that he had received my prose poem "The Song of Joan" and that it was profound. This is for Father Retter.

I heard the bells at St. James' Church ring 18 times as I crouched from a sore back on the corner with my groceries. Yes, I thought, St. James is still with me. The first three sets of three bells represent "Hail Marys" and the following nine bells are a special prayer.

I thought of the beautiful, young Japanese woman with whom I live. The number eighteen is considered very good in the Japanese culture and in the Jewish culture represents, "chai," life.

I thought of my health when now and then I hear voices, have premonitions, see lights and am in touch with the spiritual, mystical and experience the occult.

I thought of Joan of Arc who at the age of 17 heard voices and had visions; a young girl who led the French army in battle to victory but was later burned at the stake as a witch as she could not in all honesty renounce what she did firmly believe she heard and saw and because of wearing men's clothing.

I think of all those who see and hear what others do not and are, in general, neglected, misunderstood and suffer not only the torment of the mind but the torment from those who have not

walked in their shoes. I also think that, yes, it is possible, when one is traumatized, to develop a heightened sensitivity, not unlike those without sight, to experience, what others may only have an inkling, does exist.

I think of the burning chemicals (medicine) we take to lessen the trauma in order for us to be able to help ourselves and in the process, contribute to society and find venues for our energy and creativity.

I admire the tenacity, the strong survival instinct and the bravery of all those who persevere in their day-to-day living while enduring this condition.

The French have a phrase to describe the condition: "touched by madness from the presence of God."

The bells of St. James' Church are inspiring. They touch my heart, my soul, my mind and are the tears from my essence.

ANITA STEVENS
(15/7/99)

Looking or Seeing

I have always wondered what is wrong
  with me
People don't look at the heart just what
  they see
He looks too weird or funny they say
So instead they just walk away

So I have a funny looking ear and a lazy
  eye
It's the comments that really make me
  cry
Instead of retaliating, I just walk away
Just thinking that's another no friend
  today

But the time has come for the world to
  know
And it's time for me to show
The way I look is no fault of mine

During pregnancy, my mother did
  drugs and wine

I can do almost the same as you
My hair is black and my eyes are blue
I can walk, sit, and talk
I have plenty of skills in stock

Really I have a heart of gold
And very pleasant I have been told
So take the time and sit and talk with
  me
Look past the looks and see what you
  see

ANTHONY DUNNE
(1/9/99)

The Birthday of an Old Man

This old man lives in a coastal city of
BC. Two years ago he swore one thing
for himself: If he could live to 100 years
of age, he would celebrate his birthday
by parachuting from a helicopter.

Time flies very fast; he has been 100
years old since September this year.

His family is very anxious about him,
because to parachute is very dangerous
for an old man; however, he is a man of
strong will.

The helicopter took them around in

the sky for about 40 minutes. He
jumped! Fortunately he was successful
in landing.

Afterward, he told his friends that a
parachute coach hugged him tightly.
The experience seemed to cast him as an
old eagle, hovering in the sky . . . he
had a whale of a time.

SHANG LUNG LIAO (84)
(15/10/99)

Good Things About This Area, This Community

1. It is a community with a history of accepting most anyone. People are generally decent and have evolved to create the social services providing aid and interest.

2. DERA: the Downtown Eastside Residents Association was formed in 1973 to fight for basic rights in the cockroach hotels and rooming houses, e.g. sprinkler systems, doors that would close and lock, windows that would open. DERA members were instrumental in getting Carnegie reopened as a community centre. It has developed hundreds of units of housing for low income singles and families in both rental and co-op models. DERA provides advocacy services and assistance in matters relating to welfare, landlord-tenant problems, taxes and EI.

3. United We Can: a major recycling centre for many binners (dumpster divers). It provides cash for collected materials and some employment for people cleaning alleys and lanes . . . Those involved lobbied successfully to get many more kinds of containers redeemable, and United We Can now augments the incomes of hundreds of recyclers.

4. Portland Hotel Society: provides housing for people still active in addictions and substance misuse as well as mental health consumers and sex trade workers. Harm reduction and tolerance as well as psychiatric aid are part of the operation. Older hotels have been purchased and renovated to provide housing and a new hotel is going up.

5. Sun Yat Sen Gardens: an oasis in the downtown, about two blocks from Carnegie Centre. There is both a free side and an entry-fee side to enjoy the tranquility and energy in this classic Chinese setting.

6. Pigeon Park: a paved corner with trees and benches, it is an open space at Hastings and Carrall. It sits outside the base of Co-op Radio, a volunteer-run radio station whose programs and possibilities are limited only by the participants' input.

7. Victory Square: green space across the street from the downtown campus of Vancouver Community College and near the local hemporiums. The BC office of the Canadian Centre for Policy Alternatives is in the building just north of the park, providing excellent analysis and rebuttal to the machinations of the Fraser Institute. The Simon Fraser University downtown campus is about a block-and-a-half west.

8. The Downtown Eastside Women's Centre: an excellent resource for women in need of space, advocacy, food, clothing and referrals.

9. Crabtree Corner: under the auspices of the YWCA, provides assistance for single and low-income parents. There is an emergency or arranged day-care and a myriad of services.

10. Tradeworks: an established project providing the training and job search skills necessary for many to find employment. The BladeRunners program links youth with construction job sites and trades for training.

11. DEYAS: the Downtown Eastside Youth Activities Society operates the needle exchange and has direct input into youth detox, housing, and street

nurses. It works with people in substance abuse and sexual abuse situations. In conjunction with Watari, the Youth Action Coalition and the Neighbourhood Safety Office, DEYAS has made great progress working for legislation on prostitution, procurement of minors for sex and enforcement of these laws.

12. Native Health Society: front line and unique in providing medical aid, counselling, referrals and addiction services. There are a variety of projects and causes — transsexual safety, drug and alcohol programs, pregnancy options and traditional direction.

13. Evelyne Saller Centre: a community resource with a cafeteria, providing low-cost meals, recreational activities, games, pool and TV, and health services including laundry, showers and delousing.

14. Street Orientation Services: SOS is the resource centre for Latino residents, with help on immigration and refugee claims, job searches, substance abuse issues, medical network connections and ESL/job matters. The head tax and related difficulties are among the challenges tackled here.

15. Four Corners Community Savings: a financial institution created by and for low-income residents, with assistance from the legal department of the provincial government. The idea is to give low-income residents and customers the dignity and opportunities available at larger banks, trust companies and credit unions without the class or economic discrimination experienced or even inherent in such institutions.

16. Main & Hastings Community Development Society works on education for non-residents and surveys

locals to determine housing difficulties and needs. Has provided excellent housing and is seeking to develop more. Another interesting aspect is the research and exposure of the trend to privatize public space through the introduction of private security forces and bylaws prohibiting panhandling and squeegeeing (by implication, not meeting some arbitrary standard of acceptable appearance set by merchants and/or property owners).

17. Lookout: helps people find temporary shelter and emergency housing, with drop-in aid for dual-diagnosis individuals, mental-health consumers and others at the Living Room.

18. VANDU: The Vancouver Area Network of Drug Users provides peer counselling and advocacy for users in matters of housing, medical aid and needs in a harm-reduction model.

19. Various missions and churches operate programs that provide food, clothing, showers, phones, advocacy, referrals, administration of assistance money, rehab, housing and counselling.

The *Help in the Downtown Eastside* booklet contains the briefest outline of the many groups, services, agencies and organizations in the neighbourhood as a guide to what the community has. Almost every project has formed around issues like poverty, decent housing, drug misuse and substance abuse, safety, recreation, jobs and job opportunities, access to training and education, medical aid and security. These listings are, of course, limited by space and only reveal the surface. This neighbourhood is much more than just the sum of its parts.

PAULR TAYLOR

(15/10/99)

Methadone Madness

What is pathetic is she
knows she's being
cheated, given the short end
of the stick
after all it is *her* piss her
aunt uses it
to fool the doctors with
she knows her aunt uses it
to make money with
to fool the doctors with
somehow
and she knows her aunt is
making money
so why can't she have a cut?
all she wants is
maybe a chocolate bar or a
dollar or something

her aunt has got some scheme
with the doctor
— she doesn't know all the ins
and outs —
but they need her piss . . .
why? who cares?
least they could do is give her
a buck . . .
she wishes everyone wasn't on
drugs allatime
a lousy buck! it's her piss after
all.

R. LOEWEN
(1/11/99)

Christmas Eve at Muskrat Lake

On Christmas Eve
the entire village
went tobogganing
on the sloping banks
of Muskrat Lake.
Everyone was bundled up
in mukluks
parkas
mitts
and scarves.
Some came to watch,
others to ride
on this festive night
of clouds and stars.

Some toboggans scooted down
like otters.
Others slide sideways. and

still others turned over.
Tiny children
with wide eyes
were held firmly by parents
who rode with them.
Everyone who wanted a ride
found a place on a toboggan.
No one was left out.

Jeremiah, who was six,
tugged on my arm.
Come for a ride, he said,
and I rode with Jeremiah
and as many of his friends
as would fit on the toboggan.
Down the hill we went
with shouts and screams
and the toboggan skidded sideways

and we all fell off
and Jeremiah jumped up,
eyes shining,
and ran after the toboggan.

Big, fluffy flakes of snow
began to fall
from the dark sky.
Children tried to catch snowflakes
on their tongues,
and older folks stood still
and let the large flakes
land on their heads
and outstretched hands.

Gradually people started
to go home.
There were children

to put to bed,
and hands and feet
to be warmed.
It stopped snowing,
and stars were visible
among the clouds.
In the distance
a wolf howled,
and the dogs at Muskrat Lake
took up the call.

"Praise to the night and the stars,"
they sang,
"and on earth, peace and goodwill."

SANDY CAMERON
(15/12/99)

Finally!

On Friday, October 22, the Attorney
General's office announced that finally
the rice wine that has killed many of
our people in the Downtown Eastside is
officially going to be off the shelves in
corner stores and other outlets.

This lethal drug is finally being put to
rest — after seven years of struggle.
The efforts of this community have
been successful. To all who took part in
the many protests, demos and over-all
community involvement — thank you.
This community has shown a lot, not
only to us but to the whole of Vancouver.

This community has something to celebrate, and to remember those who fell
victim to this drug.

To all those who were part of this —
YOU have something to be proud of!
MARGARET PREVOST

PS: There are some groups that get a
pointed no thanks for doing a big, fat
nothing about rice wine. They include
the Gastown Homeowners Association,
the Gastown Safety Society, the Gastown Business Improvement Society,
the Gastown Merchants Association and
the Chinatown Merchants Association,
all groups that are supposedly very concerned with the quality of life in the
neighbourhood. We hope to get just as
much support from you next time, too.
JEFF SOMMERS
(1/11/99)

YOUR DRUG PROBLEM

2000

trouble

I lay in bed hearing the
horrid shrieks of someone being
   stabbed and it's no big deal . . .
common . . .
all night long violence cuts
    through the air to my ears and
    it's just part of the usual
    soundscape . . .
    the music of home . . .
    I dream of kitchens where salads
are tossed through waves of
    sitar and songbirds, yet am
grateful for charity hot dogs
    through suffering lineups that
    smell like shit . . .
am grateful for my hotel
                 room with a
tub and no roaches . . .

                        am grateful . . .
having seen what i've seen and
knowing what i know would it
be possible to lay by a
window by a quiet clean
street and ever be used to it? . . .
would gratitude grow in proportion to
    my standard of
living and would i leap naked 'cross the
    floor dialing frantically urgent 911
crying "there's trouble across
town!"? . . .
trouble in the downtown eastside . . .

JIANG CHANG
(15/1/00)

Dim gis lukws niiy – To Change Homes

On to new tomorrows . . . unfortunately that means saying goodbye to the present day. I will be leaving Carnegie to go back home to the Nass Valley. After 15 years at Carnegie, as a volunteer and staff member, I have learned a lot from all the people I have met.

When I first got here I had the "Do Gooder" attitude of being here to "fix those people," but after a few short hours I realized that I was in no way the answer to the problems of the Downtown Eastside. I quickly learned that the ignorance I had at that time did more harm than good. I would have to be more aware of the daily struggles, the abuse and neglect by some agencies and systems that were there to help.

The thing I learned about and admired most is the amount of courage and inner strength of the individuals who're here every day. I met new people, always talking about where they were going to be next week, next month, and next year. In today's world where we struggle day-to-day to feed, clothe and house ourselves, it was amazing to see that everyone had plans to do more . . . even if it was planning for tomorrow. I found that most people wanted to change to be able to help those in the same situation they were in.

Our community family spirit is more

wholesome than most others. We all feel the losses we endure and feel the highs of our new triumphs. We all want to ease the suffering that happens here, even if we go about it differently, or if some ways are more effective than others. I learned from all the people that, no matter

what happens anywhere and everywhere else, we will always have the Downtown Eastside to fall back on, to take care of us, no matter what we are dealing with and especially if we don't know how to deal with something.

I feel I have learned more from the people and struggles here than I could learn from any other centre or formal education. I will miss the centre every day and look forward to bringing the changes I have seen here back to my home so our small problems there would not add to the bigger problems here. Once again I would like to say thank you to all those who have shared their experiences and knowledge with me. I hope you all do well in whatever the new millennium brings and hope to see you further on down the road. Take care,

STEVE JOHNSON

Diamonds

When there is no love
It can break your heart
Makes you go completely
OUT OF YOUR MIND
It makes you walk for miles
And miles and wears you out
Sometimes in life you can
Lose your family and home
And even your best friend

Love can turn all of that pain
Buried deep within the soul
Like big black lumps of coal
And turn them into diamonds
THAT SPARKLE AND SHINE.

DANIEL RAJALA
(1/2/00)

My Life as a Carnegie Volunteer

In the olden days a fortress or a castle might be guarded by a dragonand/or encircled by a moat inhabited by sharks or monsters with snarly teeth who would just as soon eat you for breakfast if you hesitated or looked the wrong way. Sometimes a crafty old woman stood at the gate, offering something to eat, demanding a kiss. Falling to her enchantment is a diversion that will surely prevent you from getting safely inside the building.

Carnegie Centre is a fortress of sorts, a sanctuary, a beacon of hope and light in the dark of the inner city. The building itself has a venerable history, undergoing a thorough facelift for its latest incarnation as a community centre only just over 20 years ago. Thanks to the dedicated perseverance of far-sighted volunteers and professionals, including politicians, the building was not only saved for community purposes but also given a mandateflexible enough to accommodate the particular needs of the actual DTES community, for the most part. So we have in the heart of the place a fantastic cafeteria where the focus is on wholesome and affordable meals and a warm safe place to gather. On the same floor is a regulation-size gym as well as the newsletter office. There is the clay room, the pool and weight rooms, a darkroom and instructors for learners as well as a self-contained seniors centre on the lane level. On the main floor the theatre, with its two pianos and satisfying acoustics, shares a wall with the library, a small but well-connected branch of the Van-

couver Public Library system with grand old-style heavy wooden tables in two rooms that are usually filled with serious browsers. On the top floor is the computer room, continually being upgraded, and the Learning Centre, as well as the various offices of the always keen programmers.

Everywhere there are people engaged over board games, in lively dialogue, coming together in pursuit of a range of activities that over the years reflects the common creativity and the increasing capability of the community.

As documented in the archives and testified to by the various political luminaries who attended the recent anniversary celebration, Carnegie Centre represents nothing less than a miracle, but there are some who absolutely won't (and many who would rather not) go near this corner, surrounded as it is by levels of concentric traffic. To get inside there are perils to be faced that effectively intimidate the over-fastidious and faint of heart. For the car jocks, the gawkers and the players (and for pedestrians too) the traffic lights are venues where you get to demonstrate your attitude. Here you also get to interact with panhandlers and pushers, gentle (or not) lunatics and ruthless (or gentle) thieves. They want to sell you drugs. They want you to give them money. They know misery and can explain it. Each one has their own story which boils down to this moment, this particular urgency. They could stall you forever in sympathy. If you are alert and skilled in diplomacy, offend no one and keep an eye out for rogue drivers, you should make it easily across the street. There are statistics on the people struck down and mangled or killed on that intersection.

Safely on the corner, you are not yet home free.

A VOLUNTEER
(1/2/00)

The Carnegie Street Program in Review

It's been controversial since starting on the last day of May 1999. The Street Program has also been the subject of ridicule, praise, condemnation and heartfelt testimonials . . . yet few appreciate how much work goes into changing peoples' minds. For those who have not yet experienced the scene on the corner of Main & Hastings (and, by extension, throughout the Downtown Eastside), there are, on average, 45-50 people on this corner at the entrance to Carnegie Community Centre at any time — day or night. The majority are users and user/dealers and about 10 percent are non-addicted dealers. The population is mostly local and includes working women, homeless, drinkers and addicts withmulticultural backgrounds.

It is the largest open-air drug market in North America.

Behind this is the Carnegie Centre, the living room of the neighbourhood, which sees over 2000 individuals a day come through its doors. Access to Carnegie is open to anyone who is neither drunk, abusive nor stoned. Many of the regulars on the corner are barred from entering the building and using any of its facilities.

The Street Program staff and steering committee prepared a draft report on their reason for being, activities, direction and future plans. From page one:

> . . . to provide information, services, friendly contact for people whose alcohol and/or drug use and behaviour makes them inadmissible to Carnegie, and to create a safe space on the corner for everyone — Carnegie members, the general public and substance users. The long-term goal is to contribute towards the closure of the open drug activity at Main and Hastings.

The long-term goal will only be achievable if Carnegie and other community organizations, city hall, the health board, and the police work together in a "four pillar" approach: harm reduction, treatment, prevention, enforcement. The approach of the program is to recover the corner — now dominated by drug-dealing and drug-related behaviour — through providing a range of activities in open tents. These include:

- Information and referrals about physical and mental health and social services: via personal contact, video and print materials
- Literacy support (resume- and letter-writing, etc.)
- Cultural activities and community celebrations
- Music and entertainment
- Arts and crafts; cards and board games
- Out-trips
- Haircuts
- Aromatherapy, shiatsu massage
- Support to the street nurses (who

periodically provide inoculation and other services in the tents)

Staff have good results at times in getting users to be responsible for their behaviour. It can be frightening for members of the general public to wend their way through such a crowd, and thoughts of a larger picture and long-term goals can get lost in the face of perceived aggression or outright violence. Dealers will move if their operation is causing congestion; users will refrain from fixing in their neck on the bench while people wait for a bus; some of the dealers will not sell to kids . . . and some could care less.

Sterile observations tend to focus on what's to be seen, and there is still a strong element in favour of police sweeps every 15 minutes, 24 hours a day. Success may be a sterile word as well. The only measure is change itself, and developing positive relationships with other agencies, organizations and businesses is part of the ongoing education everyone needs, including the staff and corner people and the public.

Three long-term features of the Street Program are:

- provision of effective information and referral services
- the availability of desperately needed resources like treatment and a sobering center
- the renewal of Main and Hastings as an attractive community space

Drug addiction has damaged and destroyed many lives. The effects on a society ill equipped to handle a public health crisis of this magnitude can be devastating. The words of Dr. Martin Luther King Jr., as they applied to black people, can just as easily be applied to those who are addicted: "There is nothing more dangerous than to build a society, with a large segment of people in that society who feel they have no stake in it; who feel that they have nothing to lose. People who have a stake in their society protect that society, but when they don't have it, they unconsciously want to destroy it."

STAFF

(15/2/00)

When I Was a Crow

Cold winter dawns; we went mad with
     delight
& flew for miles without stopping
While starlings & pigeons huddled like
     beggars
'round black chimney flues & ruffled
     their feathers
Crying out with a joy we could not
     explain
Above their heads in bright chaos we
     cawed.

Blacker than night, we were children of
     morning
Tearing across God's blue eye
Our souls unredeemed, uncaring for
     churches
Abandoned to motion in any direction
& the cold air biting our wings in envy
With no protection at all we ran free.

When I was a crow
I knew what it was to be human

I suffered & died & rose up again
Crying nearer my life to thee
Crying nearer my life to thee.

& when some of us died or just
    disappeared
We were not afraid to keep flying
Cold with fatigue, our eyes on the
    sidewalks,
Our hunger unslaked
For one final flight that could not
    sustain us;

Like black empty shells raised from on
    high.

When I was a crow
I knew what it was to be human
I suffered & died & rose up again
Crying nearer my life to thee
Crying nearer my life to thee.

EARLE PEACH
(15/3/00)

In Memoriam

Officer Gil Puder of the Vancouver
Police Department died of cancer on
November 12, 1999. He had been a
police officer for 17 years, and in the
past few years he had become one of the
most intelligent and passionate speakers
in North America on new approaches to
drug control that have been shown to
increase public health and safety, and
save lives from drug overdoses and
street violence.

It took two tragic events in Officer
Puder's career before he was able to
accept the fact that the war on drugs
doesn't work. A fellow police officer
and close friend was killed on duty in
an incident involving drugs, and Officer Puder was forced to shoot an armed
drug addict in self-defence during a
failed bank robbery.

Officer Puder might have left the
police force after these traumatic experiences. He might have withdrawn into
himself, or he might have become bitter
and violent towards all those in the
underground drug culture. What he did
do was seriously study the global drug

problem, and learn about positive
approaches to drug prevention, treatment, harm reduction and law enforcement.

Officer Puder believed that the drug
crisis, which involves both licit and
illicit drugs, is a public health crisis. In
an article in the *Vancouver Sun* he
wrote, "My hope for 1998 is that Santa
has left a large measure of courage and
wisdom in a number of stockings so
that our children can mark this year as
the one when we finally began treating
drug abuse as a health issue rather than
a criminal industry . . . At some point
the policing profession must live up to
its image, place public safety ahead of
careers and take up the leadership challenge abdicated by elected officials . . ."
Decriminalization (which does not mean
legalization) would not result in heroin
sold at corner stores . . . Various drugs
(think of alcohol, tobacco) require three
different forms of regulation, which
could be phased in slowly. The windfall
savings on law-enforcement dollars
could be plowed into health care, edu-

cation and rehabilitation, which are the only methods proven to correct substance abuse. Participation (in treatment and harm reduction programs) would be much easier to encourage when sick people are not stigmatized by criminalizing their addiction . . . While millions of public dollars are squandered on the war on drugs, people continue to die. I'm tired of bringing their families the bad news."[1]

Officer Puder was a brave and caring man who spoke and wrote eloquently for intelligent approaches to drug control even when his superiors ordered him to stop. By following his example we will do honour to his name.

SANDY CAMERON
(N.D.)

1. Puder, Gil. "Dispatches from the war on drugs — decriminalize." *Vancouver Sun* 31 Dec. 1997.

Sensible Solutions to the Urban Drug Problem

Gil Puder is dead. He died at the age of 40, reportedly because of a sudden and lethal advanced cancer. Gil was a constable with the Vancouver Police Department. He gave public talks, attended conferences and was highly regarded by activists and scholars alike as an incredibly intelligent and aware individual. His views and well-researched opinions on drugs and their use/place in society and his response to them as a police officer left him ostracized and resented by his fellow officers. He was subjected to threats, condemnation, put under intense scrutiny and even recorded by delegates of his superiors on the force. His sudden death at such a young age is just a coincidence . . .

Gil Puder spoke at a Fraser Institute function in 1998. The presentation is extremely relevant to the work of this community in the "four pillar" approach to dealing with drug use — prevention, treatment, harm reduction and enforcement. The *Carnegie Newsletter* published Gil's paper over three issues; a shortened version appears here in his honour.

PaulR Taylor

Recovering Our Honour: Why Policing Must Reject the 'War On Drugs'

My belief that the war on drugs must end arises from the damage being done to both policing and the society it serves. Being a frontline police officer, I am deeply troubled by any example of counterproductive law enforcement.

While strongly believing in devotion to duty, I subordinate the unique requirements of my profession to responsibilities as a human being, parent, and Canadian citizen, who has no desire to raise his children in a country torn by needless criminality. My commitment cannot be fulfilled in a military context, applying the law in a punitive manner to people unfairly labeled as amoral losers.

Harsh, reactionary criminal justice has proven woefully miscast as a control mechanism for drug use. A truly comprehensive strategy is now required, including a legalized, controlled drug supply, coupling enforceable and decriminalized regulation with health, education, and economic programs. The challenge for policing is to measure traditional drug war practices against the integrity of truly ethical conduct.

1. Traditional Practices

Research long ago identified aggressive enforcement and a game-like atmosphere as features of drug policing, which make it an attractive field of endeavour.[1]

Make no mistake, drug-related arrests can be very easy, with hundreds of available, identifiable targets on city streets. Contrary to the Hollywood image, we rarely catch wealthy black marketeers living in mansions and driving expensive automobiles. Arrests usually involve poor, hungry people on street corners or in rooming houses and filth-strewn alleyways.

Like most professional people, we promote peer approval towards a demonstrated work ethic, and what better way to build your image than with a "bad guy" in jail, and drug exhibits or some recovered property as your visible evidence of success? Furthermore, commendations and promotion are often the result of high arrest statistics.

Over and above rewards for the status quo, there are three major obstacles to modernizing law enforcement attitudes. First, people persistently and wrongly identify drugs, rather than prohibition, as the cause of related criminal activity.[2] [Secondly,] the drug war is also a turf war, resulting in medical and criminological research being regularly ignored or discredited.

Lastly, labeling drug users conveniently removes any need for introspection about using government power to remove a person's rights and freedoms. Marginalized people simply require less respect. Turning sick people into monsters is useful for drug warriors, since it impedes serious consideration of enforcement alternatives. Abusive enforcement is symptomatic of our failure to reduce drug-related crime, yet such behaviour merely worsens a world we can't escape.

2. An Ethical Standard

Policing is one of several professions with a vested interest in maintaining the status quo. Unfortunately, money provides incentive to continue old-school practices. Line officers can earn large amounts of overtime pay generated by drug arrests. Careerists can use what may be meaningless arrest statistics as performance measures to advance their rank and salary. At the top of this continuum, managers and spokespeople have from the inception of drug prohibition publicized gang crime and drug money, pressuring elected officials into coughing up more public cash for an expanded enforcement empire.

For the overwhelming majority of officers who steadfastly perform their duty, our police self-image is too often defined by the drug war, allowing some officers the conceit that warrior-saviour is the characterization of our calling. Deified police officers confronting demonized drug users is a recipe for abuse. The most repugnant example is the unnecessary shooting of people, many of whom are unarmed. An addict robbed a bank in 1984 carrying only a replica weapon, and was killed by a bullet from the real gun I fired. Local teenager Danny Possee died in 1992 during a police raid for a small amount of marijuana, and lest anyone mistakenly believe that we actually learn from such tragedy, an unarmed Lower Mainland man was shot and killed last year, while sitting in his vehicle during a drug arrest. In war, however, both sides take casualties: I lost my friend and colleague Sgt. Larry Young a decade ago, killed by a trafficker in a cocaine raid gone wrong. Until policing expunges the politically supported fallacy that a drug war can be won, this unnecessary killing will continue.

Acknowledging when we do not know something and being humble enough to admit ignorance is the virtue of intellectual honesty. Despite the plethora of self-anointed "drug experts" in policing, who seldom hesitate to publicly volunteer opinion, I've never observed a medical or pharmacological study being referenced. Considering this paucity of true expertise, subsequent law enforcement spin-doctoring reinforces the theory that truth is war's first casualty. This intellectual dishonesty is painfully apparent when agencies appropriate the educator's mandate, substituting police for professional teachers. One only has to examine the abuses of the expensive and dubiously effective DARE program in the US[3] Extensive studies detail the failures of DARE[4] and the US General Accounting Office conspicuously declined to include the program in its recent evaluation of drug education[5]. Yet the West Vancouver Police Department is now delivering the program to local schoolchildren. I wonder if parents and local taxpayers are aware that 1998 University of Illinois research found greater drug use among students who had experienced DARE? In our information-based society we can't patronize people anymore, regardless of their age. A resurgence of marijuana use in Western societies is remarkably coincidental with electronic freedom of information on the World Wide Web, and one must ask how many teenagers now simply disregard their cigarette-smoking or alcohol-drinking parents, teachers and police as dishonest hypocrites.

If public trust is the capital foundation upon which police service is built, then we cannot afford to squander it pursuing an archaic interpretation of morality. Our professional integrity must once again remain sacrosanct.

Progressive legislation will not occur overnight, but the disastrous impact of drug war on policing is the impetus for us to demand it.

3. The Road Ahead

A critical change that must occur is our acknowledgement that drugs rarely cause crime, while money almost always causes crime. Before complaining about drug crime and the associated health costs or tax burden, people should realize that these evils are the offspring of prohibition[6]. Our unwillingness to recognize reality is an embarrassment, prompting one distinguished police chief to lament, "It's the money, stupid!"[7] By refusing to endorse a lawful drug supply which would end this black market cash cow for criminals,[8] I hope police of all ranks and agencies realize that our intransigence allows the perception of "Support your local Hell's Angel" stickers on our patrol cars. To force policing to admit that it cannot win this drug war, voters and policymakers need to "just say no" to more of the public's money for cops, guns, and jails. By responsibly allowing limited access to the relatively harmless cannabis plant, we can redirect hundreds of millions of taxpayer dollars to important social issues. Similarly to alcohol and nicotine, cannabis could be effectively controlled at the community level by regional legislation and municipal bylaws.

Regarding heroin and the opiates, the decriminalization trials in Switzerland have been such an overwhelming success, by crime, economic, health and public approval standards, that replication of the process must be implemented in this country, and none too soon. The British Columbia Chief Coroner's exhaustive analysis of illicit injection drugs finds our Canadian responses hopelessly inadequate, and in need of a broad-based, multi-disciplinary approach.[9]

I have some hope that the threshold for change has been reached, since it appears that mounting evidence is overwhelming even the most ardent drug warriors. It is my fervent desire that Canadian policing will choose the high road, placing integrity and public safety first, while shedding our traditional role of defending established interests. Perhaps the best wisdom of all comes from the minds of the pure and uninitiated, whose thoughts are untainted by a lifetime of misinformation. Viewing a televised documentary on injection drug use, including disturbing images of a man killed by his father, my nine-year-old son watched an interview with addicts who explained a myriad of disorders that were ruining their lives. Not once did he ask his father the cop why these criminals were not in jail. His advice to me was, "Dad, those people are sick." I hope someone other than me will listen.

CONSTABLE GIL PUDER,
VANCOUVER POLICE DEPARTMENT

(21/4/98)

References

1. Skolnick, J. *Justice Without Trial.* New York: Wiley, 1966. 117.
2. Alexander, B. *Peaceful Measures: Canada's Way Out of the "War on Drugs."* Toronto: University of Toronto Press, 1990. 59-60.
3. Glass, S. "Don't You DARE." The *New Republic* 3 Mar. 1997.
4. Wysong, E. and R. Aniskiewicz. "Truth and DARE: Tracking Drug Education to Graduation and as Symbolic Politics." *Social Problems* 41:3 (Aug. 1994). Cauchon, D. "D.A.R.E. doesn't work — studies find drug program not Effective." *USA Today* 11 Oct. 1993. "How Effective is DARE?", *American Journal of Public Health* Sept. 1994.
5. *Drug Control: Observations on Elements of the Federal Drug Control Strategy.* GAO/GGD 97-42, B-275 944. Washington, DC: United States General Accounting Office, 14 Mar. 1997.
6. Friedman, M. "The Drug War as a Socialist Enterprise," keynote address. Washington, DC: Fifth International Conference on Drug Policy Reform. 16 Nov. 1991.
7. McNamara, J. From "The War on Drugs is Lost." The *National Review.* 12 Feb. 1996. 42.
8. Morgan, J. and L. Zimmer. *Marijuana Myths, Marijuana Facts: A Review of the Scientific Evidence.* New York: Lindesmith Center, 1997. 6-16.
9. Cain, V. *Illicit Narcotic Overdose Deaths in British Columbia.* Burnaby: Office of the Chief Coroner, 1994.

Special thanks to Ms. C. Puder of Langley for permission to reprint this article.

Way to Go, Andy!

He's a familiar face in the Seniors' lounge, he's the proprietor of the most outrageous laugh you've ever heard, and now he's Carnegie's Volunteer of the Year!!

Yes, Andy Hucklack is getting the recognition he deserves for all his dedicated service to Carnegie and the community. Day in and day out, you can find Andy in the lane level of Carnegie, selling coffee to raise money for the Seniors' out-trips and other programs. Often, he works a double shift to make sure the coffee keeps flowing.

"He's dependable, he's always here, he never misses a shift," says Carnegie Seniors' Support Group president George Nicholas. "He's a true example of the Carnegie spirit."

Andy is characteristically more modest about his activities. "I do a little bit of this and a little bit of that," he says. "That keeps me alive and in pretty good shape. If I didn't keep doing stuff, I would probably be ten feet under the ground."

Andy has been a fixture in Carnegie almost from the day it opened as a community centre in 1980. He got recruited a few years later by Norman Mark as a Seniors volunteer. He likes it in Carnegie because "it's a place to come in out of the rain, but it's also a community where you meet new people and learn to get along with different nationalities. You can be part of something."

Ordinarily, Andy is a quiet kind of guy, but every once in a while he lets loose with a laugh that can shake the

rafters. He was born in the tiny mining town of Kingsgate in southeastern BC, near the US border, and moved to Vancouver as a small child. Over the years, he worked in logging and construction, and eventually became supervisor of a ten-member crew that handled the floor waxing at the main post office on Georgia Street. He retired from that job six years ago at the age of 65.

Andy is a life-long bachelor, but it could have turned out differently. "I was about to get married, but I got cold feet," he says. "I won't tell you how I got out of it, but I got out of it. That's all I'll say about that."

BOB SARTI

(15/3/00)

your drug problem

your drug problem
destroy others' lives

after a decade of
paralyzing depression
of psychiatrists and botched
suicides of Zoloft and Paxil
   Prozac
and meditation of working out
   and
prayer and
fasting in the woods
I finally find relief
cocaine
but you
have a problem with that

your drug problem
pushes me underground
makes me dirty
makes all my money go to
greedy gangsters and
   warmongers
instead of into health care
it goes to the vile corrupt and
   sleazy
you prohibit therapeutic use
leave me fumbling in abuse

entwined in a counterspinning culture
   of
robbery overdose beatings prostitutes
   rip-offs
illness desperation decrepitude
while the drugs
call out to children
'cause you've made them such
a big fucking deal
   cops 'nd guns 'nd rebellious
renegades
      your prison industrial complex
      your courts and lawyers and
      detox beds
      your drug problem
      destroys others' lives

my doctor sympathizes
but there's nothing he can do
he's under the thumb of you
you and
your drug problem

JIANG CHANG
(15/3/00)

Utopia

As Sir Thomas More said in his book, *Utopia*, printed in the year 1519, "If you
don't want thieves and beggars, stop making laws that create thieves and beggars."

(1/5/00)

The Whole World

If we could shrink the earth's population to a village of precisely 100 people, with all the existing human ratios remaining the same, it would look like this:

There would be

- 57 Asians
- 21 Europeans
- 14 from the Western Hemisphere (north and south)
- 8 Africans
- 52 would be female
- 48 would be male
- 70 would be non-white, 30 white
- 70 would be non-Christian,
- 30 would be Christian
- 89 would be heterosexual,
- 11 homosexual
- 59 percent of the entire world's wealth would be in the hands of only 6 people and all 6 would be citizens of the United States
- 80 would live in substandard housing
- 70 would be unable to read
- 50 would suffer from malnutrition
- 1 would be near death
- 1 would be near birth
- 1 would have a college education
- 1 would own a computer

When one considers our world from such a compressed perspective, the need for both acceptance and understanding becomes glaringly apparent.

UNITED NATIONS NON-GOVERNMENTAL ORGANIZATIONS
(15/5/00)

I Bought Her Ice Cream

How can I watch a woman I knew
In the past long ago
When she bounced on my knee
When I took her to the park
When I bought her ice cream
When I pushed her on the swing
In the past, long ago
Now, when I see her
on the corner, after dark

She is selling herself,
her spirit, her soul . . .
How can I watch
This woman I knew

PAUL WRIGHT
(15/9/00)

a thousand crosses in oppenheimer park

when eagles circle oppenheimer park we see them
feel awe feel joy feel hope soar in our hearts
the eagles are symbols for the courage in our spirits
for the fierce and piercing vision
for justice in our souls
the eagles bestow a blessing on our lives

but with these thousand crosses
planted in oppenheimer park today
who really see them feel sorrow feel loss feel rage
our hearts shed bitter tears
these thousand crosses are symbols
of the social apartheid in our culture
the segregation of those who deserve to live
and those who are abandoned to die

these thousand crosses silently announce a social curse
on the lives of the poorest of the poor in the downtown eastside
they announce an assault on our community
these thousand crosses announce a deprivation of possibility
for those of us who mourn here
the mothers and fathers and sisters and brothers
the uncles, aunts, grandmothers and grandfathers
the sons and daughters the friends and acquaintances
of those members of our community

of a thousand dreams of a thousand hopes
of a thousand yearnings for real community
lost to us but memorialized today

brought finally into a unity here in this community park
this park which is the geographical heart of the downtown eastside
these thousand crosses are a protest
against the abandonment of powerless and voiceless human beings

these thousand crosses speak to us resoundingly
collectively to warn us that to abandon the wretched
the miserable the scorned the scapegoated
makes a legitimate place for abandonment in our society
and this abandonment will go right up the social ladder
but to truly care for lives at the bottom
will make a place for care
and this caring will ensure that no one be abandoned

these thousand crosses represent the overdose deaths of drug addicts
who are not the only drug addicts in our society
but only the most visible the most naked because the poorest
but these thousand crosses reveal a culture
pretending to be about life and health and hope
but permeated with death and disease and despair
these thousand crosses bear witness not to a culture of care and freedom
but of carelessness and addiction

any one of these thousand crosses could easily represent my own death
doctors at st. paul's hospital asked me after an overdose why I was still alive?
and that is a question each moment puts to us
a question each one of these thousand crosses puts to each of us
why are we still alive? for what purpose?
our purpose is to live in community and community is care
care for one another care for those least able to care for themselves
care for all care in action
and there is no one to care if you do not care there is no one
no one at all to care if I do not care
but it would be a betrayal
of these thousand who have died to call them victims
to victimize them in death because in truth they are martyrs
these thousand crosses symbolize the lives and deaths of a thousand martyrs
the word martyr means one who bears witness
one who suffers misery for a long time one who is killed or persecuted

for adherence to a belief   an enculturated belief
that pain the pain of trying to live in this abusive abandoning crushing
and excluding socio-economic system
that this pain must be individually managed the erroneous belief
that suffering can be relieved outside real community outside care

these thousand crosses of these contemporary martyrs
bear witness not only to their drug overdose deaths
but to the uncounted deaths in the downtown eastside
deaths of drug addicts from suicide and aids

and so we are all abandoned if one is abandoned
so we are all uncared-for if one is not cared for

but if we would speak of real health and of true community
we must let these thousand crosses direct us
toward those aboriginal tribal communities and other
real spiritual communities where when one individual behaved destructively
the entire community gathered and asked one question
what is wrong with us? what is wrong with us
that this member of our community should behave in this way?

but in our culture we reverse this spiritual truth
and blame the individual solely for his or her fate
and the perpetuation of this lie costs us   costs us heavily
costs us the lives these thousand crosses represent
costs us how many more thousands of lives?
costs us in so many many ways

and from this moment here in this community park
this park of great care where the streets and alleys
and hotel rooms of the downtown eastside
the killing fields of the downtown eastside
are transformed into living testimonies and memorials
of those who have brought us together today
in oppenheimer park where children play birds sing
young people create and seniors gather
these crosses are planted like seeds in our hearts

what will be the fruit these seeds bear?
will it be a stronger commitment to compassion
and justice for every member of our community?
a commitment to those most disabled? most abandoned?

a commitment to do whatever is necessary to prevent
a thousand more deaths by drug overdose in the downtown eastside?

will these thousand crosses these thousand seeds
these thousand memorials burst forth into new life
for those who will not have to become a martyr
to our social madness around drug addiction
but will care burst forth in our hearts
in our lives in a new way for the sake of others
and for the sake of ourselves?
I believe these crosses these seeds are already bearing fruit   hope
hope stands right now right here in this park at this moment
hope is standing here hope in each cross hope in each of us

when these thousand crosses are planted in this park
who really see them are awakened
are called forth to community to care
and who really see these thousand crosses are called to be
hope soaring in the hearts of those for whom hope is gone
soaring in courage and blessing
as when eagles circle oppenheimer park.

BUD OSBORN

1997

Killing Fields

These words labeled an event held on July 11, 2000, as 2000 crosses were planted in Oppenheimer Park. In 1997, residents blocked traffic and planted 1000 crosses to highlight overdose deaths and the fact that drug users in the downtown eastside had the highest HIV infection rate in the western world. Three years later, few of the recommendations made to stop this have gotten beyond the report stage. Again, community activists and users lay this genocide at the feet of the drug-war mentality crippling all levels of government.

Three years later, drug users in Vancouver still have one of the highest HIV infection rates in the western world (VIDUS Study, Susan Currie). Between 1988 and 1998 there have been almost 2500 overdose deaths (Larry Campbell, Coroner). "It's like two Boeing 737s crashing on Main and Hastings every year"(Tanya Fader, Carnegie Community Action Project). The horror and anger of this is made more real by reading "*two* thousand crosses" throughout the following work.

CD Project Rocks Vancouver Folk Music Festival

I had the pleasure of a second-row seat on the grass at Jericho Beach to watch our own Carnegie CD Project perform on Sunday, July 16.

As the group was setting up, we loyal fans got comfortable amidst the curious, skeptical murmurs of "they're from the East Side." We were ALL in for a great surprise.

From the moment Bobby Lemieux introduced Rachel (congratulations!), until the finale with Robert Doucette, we the audience sat transfixed as, one by one, the performers hit us with solid Downtown Eastside punches.

C.R. Avery deserves the fame he is undoubtedly headed for with his powerful energy and unique drive. Even now I am on the edge of my reality seat remembering his riveting rap-mimic of drug-induced frenetics. His bold act of defiance was exemplary of one who defies convention to pierce through its veils. I have forgiven the band for their stoic restraint — hard to match C.R.'s unbridled spontaneity. To their credit, they did (finally) give him the backup he needed to carry his wave through to its tumultuous break. I hope mass consciousness was effectively pricked out of the comfortable numb state by anita stevens, who delivered a well-placed blow to the heart with her almost-Gregorian "Residential School." Anita, Rachel, Dave McC., Nancy and Bhar-bara are all out of the closet now — singer-songwriters well deserving of recognition and praise for their creativity and talent. Bharb had us all wide-eyed and stunned at the most powerful delivery of "Gad Bless the Child" this writer has ever heard. UNCANNY! BRAVO!

Robert Escott's song "Foldin' Money" had, perhaps, the greatest emotional impact for me not only from the standpoint of lyric, but also from that of his victory over a handicap that would keep many others down. Robert is definitely up, with it, and cookin'!

Lastly, enough can't be said for the unidentified (flying) bricks who make up the foundation of this golden edifice called the Carnegie CD Project: Ken, Earle, Susi, Marie-Sue Bell, Peggy, Joanne, Taum, Rudy, Dave B. Peter, John W. and RIKA (the whip) UTO. We ought to be proud of our music program, epitomizing the ideals of volunteerism — love in action, producing nourishment for the soul.

DO support these definitely-not-down-and-out-East-Enders by attending their upcoming CD-release party. Fifteen dollars will buy you the satisfaction of identifying with this soulful group.

LUKA

(1/8/00)

A Pissed Off Poem

The other night I was in deepest thought,
Pondering mightily the gravest of issues
and I mean serious stuff —
When in through my open window staggered
A big dishevelled moth, all drunk and disorderly.
At first just annoying, his fluttering
Became erratic and grew progressively chaotic.
His antics derailed my train of thought
And totally wrecked my concentration.
I got up to confront him about all of this,
But he staggered to the window and stumbled
Back into the night — and it really pissed me off
To watch him make his getaway before I had the
chance to straighten him out properly.
Standing in a rage amid all the carnage, I decided
To sift through the fragments and assemble a poem.

KEN MORRISON
(1/8/00)

Democracy in Action

Does a picture ever tell the whole story?

The Chinatown Merchants Association, the Gastown Business Improvement Society and the Strathcona Area Merchants' Society (SAMS) and a few other individuals got together to have a press conference and make statements demanding the closure of the Needle Exchange, the closure of the Carnegie Street Program and the withdrawal of funding from all agencies and/or services that support, assist or in any way aid the drug-using population of the Downtown Eastside. They demanded then that all these dollars be put exclusively into "rehab" somewhere else. We had about two hours' warning of this and the calls went around. Muggs Sigurgeirson, Jeff Sommers and Tom Laviolette went to the address only to find that admission was to the press only — if you weren't invited, you couldn't go in! All of a sudden they were inside and on the third floor of the Chinese Benevolent Association's building on East Pender. They loudly denounced the motley crew present for their narrow, reactionary response to the myriad problems in our neighbourhood. The three of them were arrested and taken out.

What the hell is this about?

Let's start with where we are — the Downtown Eastside has been given this awful rep by just about everybody, and moomentous changes are demanded everywhere. The crux of the matter is that some people want what's good for their pocketbooks, their self-images and their class. They want us — meaning everyone not of some vaguely defined level of wealth/respectability/social standing — out.

Drug users are being targeted as the most visible and, they hope, the most universally condemnable people. This is a front, the edge of the wedge. SAMS, along with various Gastown groups (one per person . . .) are vehemently and insidiously fighting to have all social services, social housing and poor people in general eliminated from "their" turf.

Expo 86 exacerbated an effect of unstated police and "holier-than-thou" policy to get all the poor and street people off Granville, out of the West End and into the Downtown Eastside. This one event sounded the bell for the greed of capital as off-shore money was lured/invited/begged-for and all the local business-driven organizations tried to intensify the massive shift to blatant non-tolerance for us being visible in their neighbourhoods. Street action, drug and alcohol use, prostitution and various other symptoms of poverty (like homelessness, even when home is a ten-by-ten-foot room) were driven into the DTES in a vain effort by

the police and holier-than-thou's to clean up their sacred site. The DTES accepted the influx of younger people, tolerated the deinstitutionalized mental health consumers being "released into the community" (given one-way tickets or bus fare to the area) and just adapted. No, this wasn't any utopia, but as a generally low-income community residents had life experiences that engendered some sympathy with others being displaced from wherever.

"Community" wasn't just a co-opted buzzword to us, but the forces of gentrification and greed and power plays began picking up speed and intensity. DERA had generated over 450 units of really decent housing, Carnegie was the living room of the Downtown Eastside, Main & Hastings Community Development and Four Corners Community Savings, Vancouver Native Health and all aspects of Native services, End Legislated Poverty and the Tenants Rights Action Coalition are in it for the long haul, the Women's Centre and Bridge Housing, the Portland Hotel Society, Community Directions, United We Can and recycling for binners and our environment, various churches have good programs, and the community of all the poor, the displaced, seniors, substance abusers and everybody are involved in getting the services that every real community needs as a matter of common sense. DEYAS began to deal with the growing drug problem, one of the most visible symptoms of societal imbalance. Youth housing, detox, bad-date sheets, sharing of info on health and a needle exchange, counselling, referrals, and other services sprang up to meet the exploding incidence of reactions.

Then the death toll began to rise. Very wealthy people took the dynamic tension and the concentration of the displaced as a business opportunity. Heroin increased in purity and availability while its street price dropped. Overdoses were rampant. Over 350 people died in 1993 and addiction grew exponentially. A report by BC's Chief Coroner, Vince Caine, listed 63 recommendations on how to deal with addiction and drug use as health problems, calling for a comprehensive system of low-key and directly accessible treatment involving not only detox but counselling, housing, and job training.

It was a light in the growing darkness. However, the forces of darkness also began to coalesce. The last thing the Gasbags want is established services and a comprehensive system of treatment that deals with addicts as people. Gastown was the first area that began to get a closed-borders mentality, with its business improvement association putting flying squads of yellow-jacketed cop wannabes on the streets harassing street people to "keep moving" and "go back where you belong." Seems that even the thousand or so residents in SROs in Gastown were unwelcome unless they just stayed invisible and paid their rent and didn't become tourist eyesores. The developer bogeyman got unprecedented concessions at shitty hall to build condos higher than anything even remotely close, to gate off public space for a private, barred no-man's-land, and name the hulk after the guy who wanted to bulldoze Stanley Park. The city-appointed Historic Area Planning Committee gets really loopy demanding colour changes on SRO exteriors and even name changes for local concerns whose monikers suggest some abhorrent affiliation with the Downtown Eastside.

The nouveau tenants and property owners in Gastown were told, as part of the sales pitch, not to worry about the street — that everything they saw outside (Pigeon Park, East Hastings, etc.) would be gone in two to three years. That yap is now *five* or *six* years old. Chinatown sees the natural outward movement of people into other areas as indicative of the failure of their marketing! Chinatown is no longer the only place for Chinese business, but the thousands of people coming every day are not enough. The fault must be assigned and what better scapegoat than the people a block or two over — the lowly street people and residents of the DTES. Strathcona gets upset over the proliferation of drugs and sex and poor people are generally unwelcome. Each of these areas gets a few people claiming to speak for everyone, and their demands are mirrored by the same vested, self-aggrandizing class interests mentioned above. Gentrification. Greed. Globalization. Class. Bigotry. Racism. Real Estate. Image . . .

About a year or so ago there was a renewed call for a "safe corridor" between Chinatown and Gastown. The rent-a-cops now prowling in relative security are seen as white (or yellow) knights, to be deployed in even greater force along one public street to keep tourists and those in search of shopping experiences safe from the undesirable influences inherent in local contact. Community people agreed to meet and discuss concerns. Those claiming to speak for everybody in Gastown brought visions of sidewalk cafes, shoppes, constant security and even closed-circuit TV. The closure of SROs on the corridor and dispersement of locals is, of course, part of their vision. DERA and Carnegie brought concerns of poverty, housing, street safety and health issues, training for jobs and local art production. After two meetings, the hardcore class junkies got fed up with listening to all this social shit and held a press conference. "Close the Needle Exchange. No more social services. Withdraw funding from any social housing or services that service, assist or support the drug-ridden, crime-ridden local population."

The matter of Woodward's is a crucial one for the future of the streetscape. The Gasbags want it to go market, high-tech, shop-til-you-drop . . . the other ten thousand or so people who like living here want social housing and surrounding empties turned into daycare and bakeries and useful stuff. The guy who bought Woodward's, Kassem Agh-tai, pulled his tricks with the community for 14 months, then when he had nowhere to hide when it came to showing the money, pulled out and has been trying to flog it ever since. Just before that, he met for a day-long "conference" with the Gasbags and was brought to his senses by Bennet and Sali and Rositch and others: the next thing was vying for a market-only development permit. Demonstrations, the infamous daisy painting, occupying law offices, holding a community celebration under the private dicks' videotape, and most recently the actions organized by the Anti-Poverty Action

Committee have pissed off the same people putting their class and vested interests forward as just "good for business."

The focal point of all this bullshit is the proposed resource centre for drug users. It's modeled on the ideas and examples of effective drug strategies in Switzerland, Germany and England. The community has held extensive and inclusive public forums and conferences, invited speakers from these programs and others in Australia and the States, and worked to get as much perspective on how to work as holistically and realistically as possible. The opposition is all out of whack. Rather than seeing the first step in treatment and

alternatives in education on safe practices and getting people inside and safe,
the reactionary right calls for treatment
on islands, in the middle of nowhere,
just GET THOSE GODDAMN JUNKIES
OUT OF MY SIGHT AND OUT OF MY
CITY.

The Mayor seemed rattled in his press
conference, held just before the one in
Chinatown, where he seemed to change
his tune, disavowing his previous support for the "Four-Pillar Approach" —
prevention, treatment, enforcement,
harm reduction — to call for a morato-
rium on all new drug and alcohol services for 90 days. The legal system gives
those violently opposed to the existing
programs another 60 days or so to
exhaust their delaying tactics.

The Carnegie Street Program is condemned for working with drug users,
for "teaching people how to be
addicts," a warped perception of teaching people how to use safely. Tables on
safe sex, on diabetes, on hep C, music
jams and board games and other activities not involving drugs are all condemned across the board as supporting
drug users. Such blanket stereotyping
gets us down to the real reason behind
everything these twerps are on about —
it's stated bald-faced in the commercial
promos of Tinseltown: "We are proud
to promote the gentrification of this
area." If you don't fit that mould, you
ain't gentry.

We respond, but it's sometimes like
talking to a five-year-old having a tem-
per tantrum. Money isn't evil, but the
things people do to get it and the effects
that pursuit of power has on them
would make a corpse puke.

PAULR TAYLOR
(15/8/00)

The Stairs

Two strangers pass by — one headed
    up, the other down,
Each absorbed in the careful navigation
    of their intricate course. — the
    tight,
twisting arc on the inside climb, marble
    treads worn into hollows over the
century — and the broad-sweeping
    curve on the descent,
And watched over by Milton, Byron,
    and Shakespeare they pass without
    comment;
The coffee stains are the evidence that
    much food and other stuff are
    freighted up;

Attempts at great feats of digital
    dexterity — two, sometimes three
    cups in
hand, or perhaps a tray laden with
    ginger beer, sandwich, soup and
    dream bars —
all wending their way to the top — And
    then there is the challenge of the
    door
that must be opened.

Many try, some succeed, and others
    deposit samples of food and drink on
    the marble;
You can do all of your business on the

stairs — they are the real Internet at
Carnegie — Catch so and so on her way
   to a meeting or holler three floors
   down,
Hear the news of a community
   demonstration, or that an oldtimer
      has found a room to live in that is
   clean and safe . . .
We celebrate on the stairs — the
   warmth and colour of the Christmas
   decorations,
the passionate red hearts of Valentines
   trimming the walls and alcoves

And the solitary flute player on the
   landing between floors two and three
   — the
magic of her music resonating up and
   down the magnificent staircase —
and percolating into the adjoining
   floors
But just what is the secret of making it
   from bottom to top? Some take it a
stair at-a-time, pausing on each landing.
   Others, more ambitious, try taking a
run, but aching knees and pounding
   chest often find them stuck
   somewhere between
two and three.

The problem is — there are a lot of
   stairs, and they seem to be at the
   wrong

Common Ground

height — half steps. So there are also
   the striders who try loping up two or
three at a time, but invariably, before
   the top, many too lose their rhythm,
and their breath — and resort to the
   step-by-step shuffle.
To strangers looking up at the challenge
   ahead — we say, "Sorry, but the
escalator isn't working today — but you
   could try the elevator!" And that is
another story.

MICHAEL CLAGUE
(1/9/00)

RAISE SHIT

2001

These Are the Faces: The Carnegie Centre CD Project

I listened to the Carnegie Centre CD *These Are The Faces*, with its 31 performers and 18 songs, over and over again. Something in me responded deeply to this thoughtful, sometimes sad, sometimes hopeful, sometimes angry music. "I know you," I said to the songs on the CD. "Yes, you know us," the songs said. "We sing your yearning. We sing what is too heavy to be borne. We sing from the heart."

This CD is a grassroots effort, conceived, planned, and fundraised by the musicians. It was recorded at the Carnegie Community Centre Theatre, where the music program takes place, and in Earle's living room.

Some people from the music program at Main and Hastings, in front of the Carnegie Centre. Photo by Renee Tabata.

Although there is a wide range of styles on the 18 tracks of the Carnegie CD, I feel a strong blues influence on some of the music. The musicians who wrote and now sing these songs know what it means to be a human being, and what a human being is up against. The pain of injustice, of exclusion, of unlived life is here, but so is the healing power of music to break through numbness and despair, and create a vision of what ought to be.

Many people were involved in the Carnegie music project, and it took three years to make the CD. It was a grassroots effort, conceived, planned and fundraised for by the musicians.

The lead singers on the Carnegie CD are Brian Cunningham, Earle Peach, Robert Escott, Mary Sue Bell, Peggy Wilson, Suzi Hollman, Rosetta Stone, Dave McConnell, Mark Oakley, Robert Lemieux, Bharbara Gudmundson, Nancy Delyzer, Rudolf Penner, Andy Costenuitt, anita stevens, Mystery Doug, C.R. Avery, Rob Doucette, and Mike Richter. The CD was produced by Stephen Nikleva and engineered by Earle Peach.

This Carnegie CD is part of the history of the Downtown Eastside — a history of struggle for human rights and dignity. Powerful corporate forces constantly vilify our neighbourhood, perhaps under the twisted notion that if they deny the humanity of the residents and the history of a community, they can destroy both the people and the place for their own profit. At the centre of our community, however, is a long tradition of resistance and caring. The book *Main and Hastings* (New Star Books, 1988) shows the strength of the Downtown Eastside. So do the Downtown Eastside poets, artists, the *Carnegie Newsletter*, and the many hundreds of volunteers in our neighbourhood. And so do the musicians in the Carnegie CD Project.

The Carnegie CD is entitled *These Are The Faces* after a song by Robert Doucette. Here are some of the words (sung to a sweet melody) that describe much of what is best in our community:

"These are the faces. These are what you look upon. We're calling all races and together we shall give so that all of us may live on and on."

SANDY CAMERON
(15/1/01)

For the Hokey Pokey Princess

Sometimes I write real bad poetry
love poems mostly stacks and stacks
of clichés, worn out phrases
cornball attempts at communication
oh I'm always sincere, sappy sweet
embarrassingly honest about
   everything
a country bumpkin in red socks
sometimes
   I'm   misunderstood
or the editor did it or I did it
but I try to shoot little missiles of
   wisdom

from my head to yours
sometimes it's pearls before swine
sometimes it's only th swine talking to
   himself
whatever it comes out as
it started with a pure heart
just got twisted somewhere on the road

AL LOEWEN
(1/2/01)

Carnegie Mission Statement 2001

Our Mission is to nurture mind, body, and spirit in a safe and welcoming environment. Through the leadership and participation of our volunteers, we provide social, educational, cultural, and recreational activities for the benefit of the people of the Downtown Eastside.

Guiding Principles

* 1. To treat one another with respect regardless of race, ethnicity, colour, religion, gender or age.
* 2. To accept and celebrate a diversity of lifestyles and cultures.
* 3. To listen and to strive to understand one another.
* 4. To settle differences and misunderstandings through patience and goodwill.
* 5. To respect the personal and private space of one another while offering friendship and inclusion in the life of the Centre.
* 6. To build on one another's strengths, skill, and natural abilities.
* 7. To contribute to the work of the Centre while enjoying the benefits of the Centre.
* 8. To ensure that people in our community are supported in finding their own voice, and in participating in the life of the Centre.
* 9. To serve the community inside Carnegie and in the Downtown Eastside.

CARNEGIE COMMUNITY CENTRE

Hopes

Confusion and fright,
Hatred and fear,
Running from evil,
The devil is near.

Looking at fun,
Wishing I had
No more running,
No reason to be mad.

The tears are leaving,
The pain has gone,
The laughter is coming,
And it's singing a song.

SHER ROBINSON
(1/3/01)

Jean-Marie . . . parti

He walked with a certain gait
Hair pulled back from a proud high
    forehead
sure footed . . . back straight.
Compassionate . . . soft-spoken . . .
    proud
We'll miss having you around
Jean-Marie parti

Je prends une bière; j'me souviens de
    toi
Jean-Marie . . . you're gone

J'regarde le monde; c'est ton visage que
    j'vois
Jean-Marie . . . you're gone

Tes douleurs sont parties mais
ton esprit est ici
T'avais déjà souffert plus
qu'un homme est capable de souffrir
Tu n'est pas le Christ

You hid your pain from us
until your pain became too much
for you to bear
Any one of us would've traded
your pain for your life.

C'est ma fête whoopee
Où es-tu Jean-Marie?

Un homme comme une femme

gentillesse un bel homme
j'voudrais que tu sois ici Jean-Marie

Ne quitte nous pas
Retient ta belle grâce
ton esprit reste ici Jean-Marie

Sans corps ça ne fait rien
dans ma mémoire tu retiens

une place
Le mot "éternité" means Jean-Marie

Prends ta bonne place mon ange, on t'a
    besoin.

LUKA JOLICOEUR
(15/1/01)

Free Jean-Marie!

they say two hundred fifty people
gathered on that day
to break bombless bread
and give voice to our will
after megaphone speeches
we nailed a plaque to the wall
then we painted up our call
give the people what they need!

the media filmed footage
the cops took photos too
lined up across abbott street
was a stolid line in blue
then folks started leaving
but some trouble had broke out
when somebody raised the call
to free Jean-Marie!

we marched to main street station
and searched the wagon windows

then we gave a badgering
to the cop what made the call
Jean-Marie there was no sight of
but the message became clear
when in spraypaint on the wall
Free Jean-Marie!

again the coppers came to bust
but we were all too strong
they could only take our paint
because our arms were linked
we answered to their questioning
in chanting and in song
the one voice of us all　　　　to free
    Jean-Marie!

S. MILLAR
(15/2/01)

To the people of your community,

A few weeks ago, we gathered to look at the video of the memorial for Jean-Marie; later we received the memory book.

How touching it is, how consoling for us. We are so grateful to all of you of the community who loved and appreciated Jean-Marie.

He probably spent the best years of his life with you all, being sober, being creative, helping other people and living in such a community.

Thank you, thank you so much to all of you.

THE BOILEAU FAMILY

The Golden Bin

Dedicated to Tom Lewis

I pray this year that I will win
The chance to dive that Golden Bin,
The Golden Bin it holds no tin —
Has coffee, brass and maybe gin
it just might hold a dream or two
A lotto ticket . . . trips to the zoo . . .
— TVs, radios, computers old,
There's just no telling what it may hold.

You'll know I found the golden bin
For on my face will be a grin,
A VCR maybe I've found . . .
A brick of gold — maybe a crown.

One thing I know I'll find no dope, but
The Golden Bin has love and hope.
It may be thick, it may be thin,
But still it will be the Golden Bin.

The Golden Bin is full of grace.
It's full of love for every race.

The Golden Bin is never locked,
The Golden Bin is fully stocked.

Maybe I'll find some boots or socks;
The Golden Bin it holds no rocks.
From the east, north, south or west,
That Golden Bin will be the best.

Unlike the uncaring city tart
The Golden Bin gives from the heart
In sun, snow, sleet or rain,
It gives and gives with no pain.

The goose that laid the golden egg
Knows that I won't need to beg
No needles in that Golden Bin
The Golden Bin someday I'll win.

MR. MCBINNER
(15/1/01)

Letters to the Editor

Dear PaulR Taylor and *Carnegie Newsletter* people:

Congratulations on another fine, successful year of putting out the *Newsletter*! I particularly enjoyed the series of articles on Rositch and the Community Alliance. If it weren't for the *Newsletter*, the truth wouldn't be out there. Please find enclosed a cheque for $— for another year's subscription to the *Newsletter*. Thanks!

YOURS SINCERELY, ROLF AUER

Dear PaulR Taylor & *Carnegie Newsletter*,

We have greatly appreciated receiving the newsletters over the past several months and feel it is the single most important vehicle around for communicating and sharing information in the neighbourhood. We would like to offer you this donation of $___ to help you to continue your fine work and would like to request that 25 (or more if you can spare them) copies be delivered to us.

THE EDGE COMMUNITY LIAISON COMMITTEE

Dear Paul,

I have just finished reading my *Carnegie Newsletter* that I received. As always, I enjoy getting it but this issue is particularly TERRIFIC. Your excellently written, clearly argued "Democracy in Action" article is wonderful. It is better than anything I have ever read in any newspaper with the odd exceptional piece in the Manchester *Guardian*. Enclosed is a token of my appreciation. Keep up the good work.

IN SOLIDARITY, PADDY

There was a decent letter from Margaret Davies that's been eaten by a file cabinet. It helps keep us on the track of the beast to know that it keeps other people inspired. It's heartening to be ridiculed and complained about and vilified as a "yellow rag" by minions of this beast, but the odd little whisper that ye olde Carnegie Newsletter is a gem, a jewel of the Downtown Eastside, keeps us inspired too.

BABA NAM KEVALAM, PAULR TAYLOR, VOLUNTEER EDITOR

Defending DERA

A scathing letter appeared in the March 1st edition of the newsletter which chastised DERA, among others, for not presenting at the development permit hearing re: the new Vancouver/Richmond Health Board proposals for the Downtown Eastside.

I would like to reply with these points: DERA reps have been at many presentations on these developments, including the first briefing session in the police department boardroom and an uptown meeting on Robson Street sponsored by the Vancouver Board of Trade at 7:30 in the morning where, as I recall, nobody else from the progressive side in the Downtown Eastside attended.

We held our February general meeting at Carnegie on February 9, with all the principals (the police, the Vancouver/Richmond Health Board, Michael Clague, and Don MacPherson) attending to answer residents' questions. We did our best to publicize the event and anyone who wished to speak to the applicants at the time could have easily done so, instead of waiting behind hundreds of other speakers in a foreign/hostile environment for many of us way across town at the Plaza 500 Hotel.

At that meeting, I voiced our concerns directly to the VRHB, most notable among them being that too few dollars were dedicated to short- and long-term detox and treatment strategies. As well, I said I thought the Roosevelt Hotel space shortchanged consumers; that it would end up being way too small to serve the people it was trying to reach

out to, and that it was still too close to Carnegie to have a substantial impact on reducing the unsavoury activities that plague the southeast corner of Main and Hastings by the outdoor washroom. As the sites had already been secured by the VRHB without soliciting advice or comment from the general public (something the VRHB has perfected to a science), it was too late by then to rectify any shortcomings even if they had wanted to.

As for the hearings themselves: Many people don't realize that development permit meetings are quasi-judicial hearings. If applicants have all their required permits in place, are working within established city policies and planning guidelines, the development permit board cannot refuse their application without risking possible legal action and suits for damages. All they can do is suggest design and other simple modifications or refer the matter to city council, which in this case had already voiced support earlier. If seven people speak in favour and 350 against, the development permit board would still be obliged to grant approval; it is not about tallying up numbers to see who comes out ahead.

Many people gave up and left unheard in frustration at the hearings and many more repeated the same comments over and over again. (We know this because DERA had observers at the hearing.)

If there's any room for cynicism through this entire process, it seems to me it should focus around why concerned people were forced to make their way to a city hall designated location rather than hold the hearing in the Downtown Eastside where changes proposed will affect people everyday these facilities are operating.

DERA continues to monitor, sponsor and participate with situations and events that affect our neighbourhood even though it may not be apparent to everyone if we don't make a major spectacle of it each time out. We are always approachable and open to criticism when it is warranted. It is unfortunate that the author of the comments found it more useful to write out a complaint without first trying to contact me to talk about these issues. Who knows, it might have saved us both time and energy in putting our remarks on paper. It might also have extinguished the possibility that our mutual enemies (we know who they are) could be chortling with glee thinking that Downtown Eastside groups are at each others' throats yet again. Maybe we all need to try a little harder to not let any more of this miscommunication infect our daily lives.

IAN MACRAE, PRESIDENT, DERA,
FOR THE BOARD OF DIRECTORS
(15/3/01)

Paranoia

I have a Safeway cart in my
    bedroom
just in case
You never know —
Life is precarious I have
    learned
One day — comfort
The next day a cold and
    rainy street and
the company of
    ragamuffins

Not that I despise the
    ragamuffins
I invent stories for their
    misfortune —
Cruel stepmothers . . .

boring prairie towns . . .
Ten Miles from the Mall.
Angels of youth angst-ridden
in these harsh interesting times.

So I keep the cart
Who knows . . . I may be next
Methinks the building manager
doth squinny at me
I did complain about the toilet
that continues
        to run cold water day and
night

WILHELMINA
(15/3/01)

Gap Between Rich and Poor Expands

The latest wealth study from Statistics Canada is convincing evidence that economic growth does not automatically help poor people. Even though the amount of personal wealth in Canada grew by 11 percent to about $2.5 trillion (net) in the last 15 years, the poorest 20 percent of Canadians lost $600 in assets. Meanwhile, the richest 20 percent increased their net worth by 39 percent, or about $112,300.

This information is contained in a new Statistics Canada report called "A Survey Of Financial Security," released on March 15. The study also shows that the poorest half of Canadians have only 6 percent of the personal wealth in the nation, while the richest half have 94 percent. This is virtually unchanged since 1984 in spite of the 11 percent increase in overall wealth. Other findings of the study include:

- The richest 10 percent of families have a median net worth (as many above as below) of $703,500. The poorest 10 percent are in debt by about $2,100.
- The average amount of student loan debt increased by over 6 times since 1984. The median student loan debt rose from $3,400 to $7,300.
- The 10 percent of families with the highest net worth hold 53 percent of all personal wealth compared to 51 percent in 1984.

If we ever elected a government that really wanted to deal with the obscene wealth gap, it would have to change laws about welfare, minimum wage, housing affordability and speculation, student loans, interest rates, and RRSP rules that benefit the middle class and rich the most, and don't help poor people at all.

While the study shows a huge and growing gap between the rich and poor, the real gap is probably much larger because the study is biased in a number of ways. For example, it probably doesn't include the richest families in Canada, like Ken Thomson, who is worth about $20 billion. Also, the study excludes some of the very poorest people in Canada: people living on Aboriginal reserves, people in jail, and residents of hospitals and nursing homes.

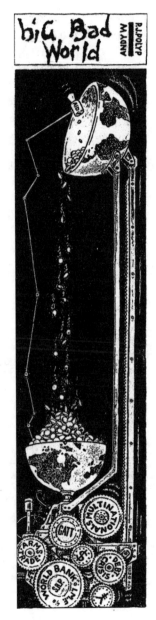

JEAN SWANSON
FROM THE LONG HAUL
(ELP NEWSLETTER), APRIL 2001
(1/4/01)

Women's Memorial March — Valentine's Day

What are you doing to end violence against women?

In loving memory of the following women:

Cheryl Ann Jo, Vera Lyons, Lorna Lambert, Rose Peters, Corrine Dagnault, Kandice Mills, Lana Morin, Bernadette Grace Peirce, Susan Jones, Beverley Whitney, Rhonda Gaynor, Nya Rane Robillard, Lou-Ann Stolarchuck (Bonnie), Corrine Sherry Upton La Fleur, Wendy Grace Lewis, Sally Abou, Debbie-Ann McMath, Vicky Buchard, Christine Elizabeth McCrae, Betty Case, Ruth Oliver, Gerry Ferguson, Jeannie Wibe, Debra Foley, Enola Evans, Tammy Lee Pipe, Melody Newfeld, Tracy Olajide, Laurie Ann Rix, Carol Ann Walden, Helen Lessardo (Bowers), Victoria Yonkers, Chantal Gillade, Dana Draycott, Amanda P. Flett (Mandy), Lisa Moosomin, Annie Cedar Jr., Rose Merasty, Maureen Riding at the Door, Meranda Isaac, Barb Mills, Beverley Ann Desjarlais, Debra Lucas, Lori Newman, Mathilda Charles, Clorissa Mary Adolph, Joyce Paquette, Darlene M. Johnston, Florence Isaac, Connie Rider, Connie Chartrand, Edna Shande, Geraldine Williams, Helena George, Karen Anne Baker, Katherine Phyllis August, Basma Rafay, Saltana Rafay, Kanwaljit Gill, Ranjit Toor, Naazish Khan, Harinder Knijjar, Swaranjit

Thandi, Linda Nelson, Michelle Wing, Peggy Favel, Rita Holy White Man, Deloris Rivet, Rhonda Macdonald, Sandra Amos (George), Janice Saul, Jennie Lea Waters, Lisa Leo, Roberta (Bonnie) Lincoln, Debbie Neaslose, Gertrude Copegop, Holly Cochran, Ruby Williams, Diane Lancaster, Bernadine Standing Ready, Pauline Johnson, Nancy Jane Bob, Wendy Poole, Charlene Kerr, Cindy Williams, Verna Lyons, Jennifer Pete, Lorraine Arrance (Ray), Sharon Arrance, Monika Lillmeier, Mary James, Barbara Charles, Tracy Lyn Hope, Veronica Harry, Susan Presvich, Barbara Larocque, Barbara Paul, Brenda George, Carol Davie, Carrie Ann Starr, Chantal Venne, Christine (Chrissie) Billy, Darlinda Ritchey, Debbie Kennedy, Maryann Jackson, Donna Rose Kiss, Dora Joseph Patrick, Elsie Tomma, Gloria Duneult (Sam), Janet Basil, Julie Mai Smith, Laverna Avivgan, Laurie Schotz, Lois Makie, Loran Carpenter, Lorna George, Lorna George (Jones), Margaret Vedan, Maria Ferguson, Margorie Susan Prisnen, Marina George, Martha Gavin, Maxine Paul, Patricia Andrew, Patricia Ann Washams (Trish), Patricia Thomas, Peggy Snow, Rose Piapst, Sadie Chartrand, Sally Jackson, Sandra Flamond, Sheila Hunt, Shirley Nix, Tanya Wallace, Terry Lynn, Jayne Hill, Verna Parnell, Alice Hall, Kelly Myers, Cheryle Joyce Vicklund, Margorie Mack, Darlene Weismiller, Michelle Lafleshe, Bernadeth Campo, Mary Anne Monroe, Jennifer Moerike, Beverly Wilson, Ruth Anderson, Janet Pelletier, Leanna Cupello, Susan Ball, June Hill, Verna Missar, Sonia Mathews, Mary Ann Charlie, Josephine Johnson, Amy McCauley, Nadine McMillan, Bonnie Pruden, Carol Davis, Mertyl Roy, Fong Min Wong and her 3-week-old daughter, Lisa Marie Graveline, April Reoch, Laverne Jack, Theresa Humchitt, Mavis McMullen.

And these women are still missing:

Dorothy Spence, Diana Melnick, Tanya Holyk, Janet Henry, Kern Koski, Sarah Devries, Sheila Ega, Catherine Knight, Catherine Gonzales, Stephanie Lane, Olivia Williams, Inga Hall, Cindy Louise Beck, Marnie Frey, Helen Hallmark, Angela Jardine, Marcella Creison, Kathleen Wattley, Elaine Allenbach, Julie Young, Ingrid Soet, Andrea Fay Borhaven, Jacqueline Murdock, Michelle Gurney, Jacquilene McDonell, Taressa Williams, Sherry Lynn Rail, Jenny Furminger

and how many more?

trust

i
trust
people
'til
they
cross
me
and
then
they
owe
me
their
souls

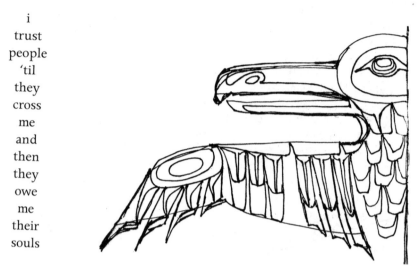

ANITA HAVIVA STEVENS

(1/6/01)

Bridge Housing Society for Women

Dear friends & families of the Downtown Eastside,

The Bridge Housing Society for Women is proud to announce the opening of our new building at 100 East Cordova at Columbia. It is a dream that has been carried for over 26 years by different groups of women. We would like to thank the community and all those who have believed in and supported us in this dream.

The building will house 36 women in permanent apartments; provide short term stay for 12 women and we are renting the basement and the main floor to the Downtown Eastside Women's Centre

for a few dollars per year. We have hired ATIRA (they run transition housing for women) to manage the building so call them at 684-3571 with any questions about tenancy. The rooftop has raised gardens, a common room and will be home to the Bridge Society office. We will be having a grand opening in the fall once all the details have been worked out and then we will invite you all to join us for a tour. This is truly a community success story.

ELLEN WOODSWORTH

(1/6/01)

The Dugout

It's a storefront situation in the unfortunate area of Gastown, at 59 Powell.

I first got involved with the Dugout in 1990. It wasn't for free coffee, bread, soup, or to watch TV.

1990 was the first time I decided I needed help — for alcoholism. Every day at 12:30 pm there's an AA meeting. My brother came to my home every day for a month, exactly at 12:15. He introduced me to this program.

From that year on I felt good. I faced my so-called fears, and years of abuse. It wasn't easy, but you know in order to heal from the inside out . . . if I didn't do this I could be dead. During 1990 I found a peace and happiness — it's called finding a form of belief.

I choose to call this belief my Creator — the eagle who flies high in the sky of the Downtown Eastside.

The Dugout is a safe haven for many people.

The Dugout has been condemned by people claiming to belong to the Gastown Business Improvement Association (GBIA). They have used their influence to pressure the city to get it out, even though it's doing great service to local residents. Just recently the Dugout held an open house for the purpose of showing the GBIA and others in the neighbourhood just how it works and who uses it.

Guess what? They never showed. Shame on them.

A FRIEND OF BILL W.

(1/6/01)

The Dugout is a Decent Place.

Community Directions —
Working with the Downtown Eastside

Community Directions is a coalition of residents, and over 40 organizations, determined to defend the Downtown Eastside from those who want to push us out.

When the Governor General of Canada visited us on March 10, 2000, she saw our pride and our strength, and she compared the Downtown Eastside to a lively small town. She could see and hear us. We hope that Community Directions can help to build a united voice so that government, the media and the wider Vancouver community will also see and hear us.

Community Directions works to find neighbourhood agreement on important issues. It only puts forward positions on social issues that have wide community consent. Each person in the coalition respects the opinions of other members, and all members, and groups, agree on certain principles. One such principle is "that all people have the right to a voice in making decisions that affect their lives."

Community Directions has six working groups, and the working group on alcohol and drugs has developed a comprehensive community plan to address the drug problems in the Downtown Eastside. Many reports on drugs have been written over the years, but what makes this plan unique is that it has been entirely envisioned, developed and written by the people of the Downtown Eastside community.

The plan is the result of over a full year's work. Two all-day community think tanks were held, and they formed the basis of the alcohol and drug plan. Ideas from the think tanks were discussed and expanded in numerous community participation workshops, and the plan is now being brought back to the community from which it was developed for a complete review. A basic insight of the plan is that drug addiction is a serious health problem, not a criminal one.

The Community Drug and Alcohol Plan focuses on four areas: (1) *prevention*, including positive alternative activities for youth and a realistic community-based drug and alcohol education program; (2) *harm reduction* that reduces the harm of drug use to the community and to individual drug users; (3) *treatment* on demand, and an increase in the variety and amount of programs; and (4) *enforcement* that is community-based, and involves an active partnership with the police department.

The plan also divides needed services into three categories: low-, medium- and high-threshold. Low-threshold services are those targeted at people who are not ready or interested in treatment or rehabilitation. These include services such as the needle exchange and supervised injection rooms, aimed to keep people off the street and enable them to stay alive and well until they get treatment.

Medium-threshold services are those that would require a degree of commitment from the user, and therefore include such programs as detox, methadone maintenance or heroin maintenance.

High-threshold services are those that target addicts who want to exit the drug scene completely, and include treatment programs and recovery houses. The low-, medium- and high-threshold services will address the spectrum of those currently living with drug and alcohol addiction, ultimately benefitting the wider community.

The plan is comprehensive in its approach, and requires that equal emphasis be placed on prevention, treatment, harm reduction and enforcement. The plan also requires that these four areas, and the three categories of low, medium and high thresholds, be implemented together. This comprehensive implementation is essential for the drug and alcohol plan to be effective.

COMMUNITY DIRECTIONS
(1/6/01)

Dan Feeney, Expertise and Political Judgement

In his article "Downtown Eastside pro forma" (*Carnegie Newsletter* 15/4/01), Dan Feeney warns us of the danger of experts who come to tell us what's good for us, and he is dismayed "that the idea of expertise is so ingrained as to be indistinguishable from, say, breathing." Dan is right. In our fragmented world of specialists, expertise has become too closely associated with power and control.

"We are managed, not governed," Ursula Franklin said. Experts presume to know what is best for us. They measure us with their slide rules, and turn us into numbers. True, mathematics is the language of technology and business, but it is not the language of human beings trying to make sense of their experience.

Managerial elites manage us with technological skills that stress efficiency and cost-effectiveness. Their world involves systems and quantification, and is far removed from the real world of suffering people. The introduction of a hostile management culture into welfare offices is a good example of expertise gone mad. Experts figured out that a vicious dog approach to people seeking help could bring about a 6- to 10-percent decrease in welfare caseloads. This brutal approach undermines every decent thing our country is supposed to stand for, and turns welfare offices into centres of rage and distrust — much to the dismay of welfare recipients and social service workers.

In the twentieth century, large administrative systems and sophisticated technology have distanced people from each other. Governments and senior officials (experts) have become so removed from the reality of poor and unemployed citizens that they have ceased to see them as human beings. They don't seem to be aware of the anguish, despair and anger that impossibly low welfare rates and draconian consent forms can cause. They tend to see the people they're supposed to be helping as stereotypes, and therefore

Waiting for the wake

non-human, and in falling into their official expert role, they become non-human themselves. Rationality and efficiency, taken to their logical conclusion, lead to the criminalization of poor and homeless people, and then to Auschwitz and the Gulag.

Bureaucratic culture (both private and public) sees society as an object of administration, a collection of problems to be solved, a garden to be weeded, or a resource to be exploited. Morality, in the context of management, becomes the commandment to be a loyal, efficient and diligent worker.[1] Adolf Eichmann was all of those things.

Expertise, as technological decision-making, tends to separate reason from feeling, rationality from living experience and efficiency from ethics. The society that surrenders to the rule of technology, the rule of the expert, will eliminate the human face of the other — the one who reaches out to us. Citizenship is the antidote to expertise. Citizens,

not experts, fought to end the Vietnam War. Citizens, not experts, worked to curtail the nuclear industry. Citizens, not experts, fought environmental pollution. Citizens, not experts, fought against the freeway project that would have destroyed part of downtown Vancouver. Citizens, not experts, fought to save Strathcona from high-rise mania. Citizens, not experts, are fighting to protect all peoples from the imperial globalization of the transnational corporations.

Citizenship is an expression of our deepest need for each other and for the land. Citizens believe they can build their community in such a way that all persons will have the opportunity and resources to live fully. Citizens uphold the common good which is democracy, and they exercise their political judgment to carry forward this vision of liberty, equality and community.

Political judgement looks at the decisions we need to make as a community in the light of all that is meaningful to us in our history and traditions. It is a form of public seeing that sees because it cares, and it moves beyond the coercion of specialization to the wisdom of shared experience. Dialogue is essential to political judgment, and dialogue requires mutual respect and intense listening.

Farrell Toombs reminds us that dialogue is impossible when one person thinks he/she knows what is best for the other, and he says, ". . . we fail when we attempt to train experts to correct the situation of subordinated persons. Our only course is to question our own fundamental assumptions together . . ."[2]. As Lila Watson, an Aborigine Elder from Australia, has said, "If you have come to free me, you are wasting your time. But if you have come because your liberation is bound up with mine, come let us work together."

And come, let us talk together and exercise our power of definition, whether it be through the committees of the Carnegie Community Centre Association, the committees of Community Directions, the *Carnegie Newsletter*, the *DERA Newsletter*, the Downtown Eastside Poets, the Downtown Eastside musicians, Four Corners Community Savings, VANDU, the Portland Hotel, the Downtown Eastside Women's Centre, the Downtown Eastside Seniors, the Interurban Project, or any other group that meets together and supports its members for the common good. "Language is always the crucial battlefield," Benjamin Barber said. "Left to the media, the bureaucrats, the professors and the administrators, language degenerates into one more weapon in the armory of elite rule."[3]

1. Bauman, Zygmunt. *Modernity and Holocaust.* Cornell University Press: 1989.
2. Toombs, Farrell. *For Every North American Indian Who Begins to Disappear, I Also Begin to Disappear.* Toronto: Neewin, 1971.
3. Barber, Benjamin. *Strong Democracy.* Berkeley: University of California Press, 1984.

SANDY CAMERON
(15/6/01)

Local News

On a much lighter note, kudos and a loud "Yes!" to Carnegie staff who went to Oppenheimer Park on July 22 and pulled the plug. On what? Some front organization for a multi-millionaire evangelist from Korea asked the park board if they could have an "event" in Oppenheimer Park. No mention of religion, no contact with Carnegie, no interest in any other schedule or use. The plug got pulled on the "Holy Fire Miracle Crusade" of Cho Suk Lee and his Healings & Deliverance & Signs & Wonders. Some holier-than-thou demanded non-interference with "God's work" (sic) saying that "This area needs us!!" The response by one staff member, slowly, as if speaking to a four-year-old: "I Don't Need You."

STAFF
(1/8/01)

Mosaics of Our History

1. The Mosaic Project is great: Tuesday, August 7, marked the official "opening" of the 17 mosaic markers that have been created and inlaid in sidewalks throughout the Downtown Eastside.

2. The Old Vancouver Townsite Walking Tour is the name given to enticing people to stroll in our community, with a guidebook bearing the same title, and see the rich history and events that mark our heritage.

3. The Living Footprints Community Art Project is the unique catalyst that provided the foundation for this — a project with the aim of creating beautiful markers that depict history, events, people, places and spiritual ideas, all with a tremendous dedication to local talent, volunteers, artists, and at the core the Carnegie Community Centre with staff and members working together.

4. The Vancouver Agreement is the accord between the municipal government of Vancouver, the provincial government of BC and the federal government of Canada to work on such nefarious ideas as "revitalization" and "economic development" and "cleaning up" — the Downtown Eastside. It gets funding and staff support and kind words from the three levels, and residents keep working not to be overlooked in the plethora of projects and ideas and consultants getting the lion's share.

5. Western Diversification is where the money came from: it's a federal program and put $200,000 in. It was administered by Carnegie Centre, and went to artists and supplies and facilities and stuff. I expect that a financial report is public knowledge, and they've come back asking that another proposal be submitted in order to continue this work! Yeah! Seems that the potential of these mosaics and the tour being a great and valued addition to the diversity of our neighbourhood has prompted several locations (and their attendant happy campers/businesses) to try "commissioning" sidewalk mosaics in front of their domiciles.

6. Gastown, Powell Street, Strathcona, Chinatown, Victory Square . . . is the list of areas that are referred to in the text and on the tour of the promotional booklet. It was available at the ceremony held in Oppenheimer and referred to by speakers as something everyone could get. Then it hit us (us being local people) — nowhere on the cover nor in the entire book were the words Downtown Eastside.

Questions were asked, and it seemed to smack of the ongoing classism and promotion of gentrification that the business groups in Gastown and Chinatown and Strathcona have been pushing for a few years. It's not a head-butting confrontation, but the Downtown Eastside has been struggling for years to be recognized as a vibrant and dynamic community, unique and vital, and the above-named areas are all a part of, not separate from, this Downtown Eastside community.

The Carnegie Community Centre Association is the prime sponsor and instigator of the project, and asks to have our community, the Downtown Eastside, named on both the map and cover of the guidebook. What at first seemed to be sinister (or just snotty) was rationalized by people being away when the final draft of the booklet came in for approval, there was a deadline, etc. Innocuous enough. The remedy is to have stickers affixed to the covers of all books already in print (about 2000) that have the words "Downtown East-side Community" above all the sub-districts named, and covers for any subsequent printings changed to include these words in the original.

The sticker solution has a precedent. Another oversight was remedied by affixing one to the inside back cover. It tells one and all that there is, in Oppen-heimer Park, a mosaic with a bench on top dedicated to volunteers who've died.

Maybe the axiom here is "The first shall be last."

The artists who worked on this project were: Pat Beaton, Taki Bluesingei, Joe Bolton, Jane Cameron, Jacquie Dionne, France Guerin, Dan Hill, Katie Johnson, Des Media, Anne Marie Slater (Artistic Director — banner program), Anthony Sobala, Marina Szijarto (Artistic Director — mosaic program), Candace Wagman, Bruce Walther, Gweny Wong and Debra Yelva. This project would not have been possible without the efforts and time of innumerable volunteers.

PAULR TAYLOR
(15/8/01)

Who Knew

Who would've thought I'd end up in here
Who would've thought I'd go down for robbery
Who would've thought I'd fight over the phone
I really never thought I'd be so alone
Who would've thought I'd be a mom
Who would've thought I'd be a widow so young
Who would've thought he'd leave me with HIV
Yeah that's me

SHERRY ALLEN
(1/11/01)

Vision Quest 2001

You might have seen a tipi and several tents and blankets in Oppenheimer Park, next to th totem pole, from August 14-18. It was a fast to bring attention and some answers to th problems our First Nations people deal with daily. During those four days, 12 people camped in th park without food, drinking only water. Th tradition is to go to a mountain or a hill alone, to sit in one place and stay awake as long as possible without food and sometimes without even water. It's a search for guidance. Th answer comes through physical suffering and prayer, in dreams, tears and often a visit or a vision of a spirit-helper. "A different type of knowledge than you get from watching TV or reading th newspaper," Edna Brass says.

Edna, one of th elders and core members of Vision Quest, explained why they do this in th city. It's to see th alcoholism & addiction, th dis-ease, th poverty & prostitution, th role th police and th System play, and to remember th loved ones who are missing or murdered. It's both a ceremony of survival and a wake-up call. People come for different reasons: for strength, physical, emotional, mental and spiritual; in protest; and in prayer. Edna chose a spot to set up her tent surrounded by th beauty of th trees, and cleansed and blessed it with sage and cedar. She says, "To Native people, every green space is a church, and it's time we started using those churches whenever and wherever we can. For many Native people living in th city, traveling to th country and climbing a mountain just isn't possible."

Vision Quest's first fast was in 1998 in Pigeon Park. They chose a place where th hurt and abuse are so obvious, including abuse from th System. Many Native organizations were invited to participate, but no one came. Four people spent four days and nights in what is considered "th worst place" in Vancouver, sleeping on th ground "which is where many of our people end up sleeping anyway," Edna said. This fast was named "From th Cement Up" and was th event that strengthened her, among others, to become a spokesperson for urban Aboriginals, to encourage everyone to get up, speak up and make a difference, to open their eyes to what is happening in our neighbourhood, and to recognize all people that are missing and murdered.

Last year's Inner City Vision Quest was at Victory Square, where a monument reminds us "Lest We Forget." One of th elders said, "It is a place where we can come together to publicly mourn those lost and wounded in th war against our identity, while sharing and coming together in search of a vision for a better tomorrow."

This year's Vision Quest started with 12 fasters. Ten made it through th whole four days after two of th men doing security were caught by an elder munching on a Kit Kat chocolate bar on th second day!

I was one of th many supporters who dropped by with water, and was greeted with hugs, teasing and laughter. I was introduced to daughters, nieces, aunts and friends. I joined th other women singing th Women Warriors' Song from Lillouet, th one we sing

on th February 14 March for our women in th Downtown Eastside. People stop and ask why we're here, what's it all about? There's no brochure, just a simple banner, and questions are directed to an elder. She explains that this is a non-violent gathering, a traditional ceremony, like a Sun Dance or a Rain Dance. "There is genocide on our streets. Why is it always about greed instead of need?" She explains that she is fasting for those living under th threat of starvation, and that she is fasting because of th epidemic of residential schools and child apprehension. She was a prisoner of residential schools for 10 years herself.

As if we needed more proof of this, one of th women supporting th fasters brings her baby that's in foster care to th park on a day she has a visit, and th social worker shows up, criticizing her for bringing her child where there are alcohol and drugs, seeing only a portion of what is going on in Oppenheimer Park. Everyone was so upset. Apparently she ignored th explanations of th elders that th mother was participating in a traditional sacred ceremony, and had only seen as far as her own prejudices and fears. It was unclear when she and th woman and her baby left th park whether she had refused th mother any more visits, as she had threatened.

Th fasters didn't sleep well th first night, and found out from security in th morning that th police had pulled a gun on some of th other people using th park. I heard horrific stories of family members threatened and brutalized by th police, as well as those who had died in jail.

Matthew Coon Come, national chief of th Assembly of First Nations, stated last Sunday that "within Canada there are two realities. There is th 'reality' of a highly developed, just society that th world knows, and then there is th harsh and deadly reality which aboriginal peoples endure. Racism against indigenous peoples in Canada alone, direct and systemic, costs thousands of lives per year." Amnesty International reports on human rights abuses, and this year they included the Ontario Provincial Police's 1995 killing of Dudley George and Saskatoon police dumping aboriginal men outside city limits in sub-zero weather last winter. Many Vancouver Natives can complain of similar treatment, including a daughter of one of th women at the quest.

During th fast, police were called to take a knife off an elder who was carving with it. They totally disregarded that th place where a ceremony takes place is sacred. One of th men doing security spoke up: "Why is it OK for white men to come and screw up our Native ceremony? But what do they do if Natives go into a Christian church and tear up a Bible?!"

On th third night many of us had powerful visionary dreams. We got together and talked about them th next day. As well, I wrote mine down, and a friend drew three pictures of what he'd

seen. We didn't jump out of bed, grab a coffee and run out th door! We recognized we're living in a world where everything is sacred and full of meaning.

Edna, who ran independently in th last federal election, calls herself a feminist. "I am liberated, I am authentic. How do you get it out there? How do you get people to listen to you?" As with addiction and recovery, we can only "carry th message." This was made painfully clear by her drug-addicted daughter's visits to th camp, when Edna's gentle yet powerful love for her was obvious to me, as she repeatedly suggested th woman lie down in her tent and sleep. Edna is raising her 11-year-old granddaughter Cheyenne, because her daughter can't. Cheyenne participated every day in th fast, but went home to sleep and eat (as I did!). On th fourth night we started to celebrate, knowing it would all be over soon enough, and Cheyenne whirled and danced in a blanket, th star of th show in th centre of our circle, then afterwards laughed, offering to teach th adults how to dance.

On Saturday th fast was broken with drumming & blessings & blueberries, before a feast of salmon, moose and bannock for everyone. Though I have asked, I still don't know if th elder got his carving tool back, or th mother got her baby back. I do know it was a powerful healing ceremony for everyone involved and am honoured I have been chosen to write this for th Carnegie Newsletter.

DIANE WOOD
(1/9/01)

A Doorjamb's Edification

She straggled up the front steps
    slowly and studiously.
She sauntered next to me
    I could smell booze on her breath.
"Ma'am," I said, "I can smell alcohol.
    Have you been drinking?"
"Jerk! Asshole! Fucking Goof!" she
    yowled odiously
I was stupefied.
I was polite, she responded rudely.
Fortunately for me, she turned away
    and
                she started to walk down the
steps
Then I heard . . . thud . . . thud . . . thud
    . . . whap.
She had been tripped by that egregious
    worn down
front step: It's an excellent
    breathalyzer.

Jarred from my stupefaction, I
    wondered:
        What the beep beep do I do now?!

If I help her up, she might be rude to
    me again;
she had bruised my thin skin . . .
I waited.
She didn't move for what seemed like an
    eternity.
I ambled to her aid — very slowly —
    she could bark at me again.
I helped her to her feet.
I asked, "Ma'am, are you OK?"
    She flashed a smile
"Thank you," said she with esprit de
    corps. Off she promenaded,
west on Hastings, into the early fall
    morn

*Eight years later this story tickles me. I
had learned, first-hand, about public
service — Carnegie style. All you do is the
following: ego suppression, wait one
minute, and a foe becomes a friend.*
        MIKE GUY — A.K.A. SLACKER
            (15/9/01)

Raging Grannie

Dear *Carnegie Newsletter*,
    PaulR Taylor's article, "Conspiracy",
on tax and service cuts, was right on
the nose. And you're right; they are
NOT liberals. They should call themselves Gliberals because they say one
thing and do another. One of the most
blatantly cynical examples of this came
just this Monday, the first day of a pub-
lic-relations gimmick by the Liberal
government, "Affordable Housing

Week." On this very same day, George
Abbott, the minister for housing and
everything-else-that's-of-no-value-to-
the-Liberals, announced that the program was to be gutted and 12,000
projected units were to be shelved. I
wrote an angry song about it that day.
    The next day was the official opening
of the Bridge Housing Project. (Way to
go, you guys!) All the nobs, including
representatives from the provincial gov-

ernment, turned up to take credit for a very fine job. Still, I think most people knew that the success here was due largely to the tremendous amount of work that was done by local people over the last two to four years.

Well, on Tuesday we were a small group of old women who had been invited to sing. We had a bunch of songs congratulating the tenants and workers of the Bridge. When we were going over the line-up beforehand in the lobby, we also ran through the new song about cuts to social housing. A government bureaucrat of some kind heard us, got pretty steamed up, and told us we were not to sing that. So we didn't, not wanting to spoil a happy occasion anyway.

But two things have stuck with me from that day: One was when a young tenant was talking to us all in such a moving way about what the Bridge shelter had meant to her, and I could have cried for all of the people whose chances for such housing have now been cut.

The other was Sandy Cameron's reminder in the *Carnegie Newsletter* of Shakespeare's "Speak what we feel, not what we ought to say." So, here is that song on . . .

Affordable Housing Week

Tune: "You Made Me Love You"

George Abbott tells us,
Verse:"I didn't want to do it —
(the Gliberals made me do it)
— Cut social housing."
He says that they'll "review" it
Which means they really blew it.
We'll lose twelve thousand units
For Housing Week!
Twelve thousand homeless
Can stay out on the street.

George Abbott tells us,
"Because of cuts in taxes
We'll hone up all our axes
And cut such 'perks' as

Housing for the poor,
and then
We'll cut and cut
some more."
Mister Abbott, we
could cry for
You're holding back
the housing
that these folk could
DIE for
George Abbott, we're
watching you!

**[RAGING GRANNIES &]
JOANNA NAGEL**
(1/11/01)

Mould and Money

I am a middle-aged woman who, unfortunately, has found herself at the mercy of government assistance. This means also that I have the unfortunate circumstance of standing in bread lines and frequently "free food" lines and outlets.

I am not an ungrateful woman. I appreciate all that is given me; however I feel that it is high time someone said something as to the quality of food given. All too frequently I receive rotten, damaged, mouldy and outdated food products that would not be ALLOWED to be sold in local supermarkets. Am I to be grateful because it is free and consume these unsafe products?

When Jesus said, "Feed my flocks," did he mean give them that which you would otherwise throw in the garbage?

Canada's Food Guide to Healthy Eating says that one should consume five to ten servings of FRESH fruit and vegetables, as well as several other servings of grains, meat, milk and milk products to achieve maximum health.

My (and thousands of others') Income Assistance does not support this guide; therefore my (and thousands of others') health is compromised.

Bad food is dangerous . . . that is why it is removed from supermarket shelves. Unhealthy bodies = unhealthy minds.

ELIZABETH ASHEFORTH
(15/10/01)

Globalization and Poverty as Violence Against Women

On September 11, 2001, over 35,000 children died from starvation in poor countries around the world. While the mass media focused completely on the tragic deaths in New York, thousands around the world who were also dying because of a violent economic system were ignored.

Poverty may not sell as many newspapers as terrorism does, but it is even more deadly than terrorism. All the time. Poverty kills more people, especially women and children, around the world.

In the so-called global economy, which some have called the casino economy, we are seeing the rich get richer and the poor get poorer faster than ever before. According to the United Nations, the income gap between people in the world's wealthiest nations and the poorest nations has shifted from 30:1 in 1960 to 60:1 in 1990. It jumped again to 74:1 in 1997.

Globalization continues the pattern of exploitation that imperialism and colo-

nialism began. For centuries the North (by which I mean
countries like the US and Britain) has been stealing the
resources of the South (by which I mean countries in Africa,
Asia, Latin America). This was first done by governments
and is now continuing under multinational corporations.
People have been forcibly and systematically pushed off
their lands and impoverished, both here on the First Nations
land we call Canada and around the world.

If we keep this situation in mind, the migration of people
across borders is a political act for it rejects the impoverish-
ment and exploitation that global corporatism inflicts on
large populations around the world. Why is it that only
wealthy people are able to move across borders so freely?
Poor people should have that right too. Why should a
woman in China make two dollars a day sewing clothes for
12 hours when she can make seven dollars an hour here in
Canada sewing clothes? Either way, she is still poor by Canadian standards.

It is important to remember the history of why and how
some people became so poor at the same time that some people have become so obscenely rich . . . To have several cars
and houses all over the place is obscene when people around
the world are still dying of starvation.

Over one billion people worldwide struggle to survive on
one dollar a day or less. Over one billion people don't have
access to safe drinking water. About 150 million children are
malnourished, and more than 10 million children under five
will die in 2001 alone. In Iraq alone, an estimated 5,000 children are needlessly dying each month because of sanctions.

There is enough food for everyone on this earth, but it is
not properly distributed. One-fifth of the world's population
controls over four-fifths of its resources. This is immensely
violent, and we see the effects everywhere from here in the
Downtown Eastside to the thousands of deaths of children
every day around the world. This is a global tragedy because
there's enough wealth on this planet to prevent these deaths.
The question, however, is one of political will. I hope to see in my lifetime a society
that addresses the deadly effects of the current economic system instead of wasting its
resources on needless war.

RITA WONG
(1/11/01)

Between the Lines

I picked up the October 1 *Carnegie Newsletter* from the lobby and briefly gazed at the cover. It took about five seconds to assimilate the significance of the cover that showed "Wanted Dead Or Alive" posters of people who go against the grain of the USA's politics and foreign policies.

A few weeks later I picked up the October 15 *Newsletter* and read that the front cover of the October 1 issue had been equated to hate literature by the editor of an ethnic newspaper!

Upon analyzing the confusion of perceptions between my impressions of the front cover and that of the editor, I came to the conclusion that regular readers of the *Carnegie Newsletter* have been elevated over the years to an almost esoteric state of understanding, while a novice reader might look through the *Newsletter* and wonder what on earth's going on here!!

What I believe this cover, along with several articles on the same topic, reflected was a desire to cease aggressions of violence and to negotiate a peace with our perceived foes.

If the editor of the newspaper missed the point of the front cover of the October 1 *Carnegie Newsletter*, then it is strongly recommended that he become a regular reader in order not to go off half-cocked with hurtful accusations of hatred.

GARRY GUST
(1/11/01)

Poverty in the Promised Land

In the Fifties we scrounged the dump
    for heavy glass
— pop bottles — coca cola, orange
    crush, 7Up —
Patsy Murphy & I traded them for
    penny candy:
Black Babies, Honeymoons, Coconut
    Buds,
        — tiny cones full of honey +
    brown sugar — delicious to us.
Also the blackberries by the train track
    —

Near the dump, the abattoir &
    Africaville; but
the biggest, juiciest grew near the
    graveyard . . .

We sold them for 50¢ a quart (remember
    quarts)
Now I cruise the lanes for good garbage
    cans + bottles for recycling —
to buy bread & milk, maybe a little
    meat

Oh Canada, our home + the Native's
    land
Glorious and free!
Freedom is a thin gruel
Human rights cold comfort in the mean
    streets.

WILHELMINA
(1/12/01)

raise shit — a downtown eastside poem of resistance

"the myth of the frontier is an invention that rationalizes the violence of gentrification, and displacement"

— **NEIL SMITH**

"these pioneers in the gradual gentrification of the downtown eastside say their hopes for a middle-class lifestyle are undermined by the tenderloin scene down the street"

— **DOUG WARD, 1997**

"prominent amid the aspects of this story which have caught the imagination are the massacres of innocent peoples — atrocities committed against them and, among other horrific excesses, the ways in which towns, provinces, and whole kingdoms have been entirely cleared of their native inhabitants"

— **BARTOLOME DE LA CASAS, 1542**

there is a planetary resistance
against consequences of globalization
against poor people being driven from
    land
they have occupied in common
and in community for many years

and while resistance to and rapidity of
global gentrification
differs according to specific local
    conditions
we in the downtown eastside
in the poorest and most disabled and ill
    community
in canada

are part of the resistance which includes
the zapatistas in chiapas, mexico
the ogoni tribe in nigeria
and the resistance efforts on behalf of
    and with

the lavalas in haiti
the minjung in korea
the dalits in india
the zabaleen in egypt
the johatsu in japan
and these are names for
the flood
the abandoned
the outcasts
the garbage people
the homeless poor
and marginalized people

and gentrification has become a central
    characteristic
of what neil smith perceives as
"a revengeful and reactionary
    viciousness against
various populations accused of
    'stealing' the city
from the white upper classes"

and this viciousness and violence
brought to the downtown eastside
by friendly predators
such as builders planners architects
    landlords

bankers and politicians
is like violence brought to our
    community
by other predators
by johns and oblivion seekers
by sensationalizing journalists

by arrogant evangelizing christians
predators like
developers and real estate agents
who remind me of no one so much
as gilbert jordan
the serial killer
who came down here repeatedly
and seduced bribed and bullied
10 native women
into drinking alcohol until they were
    dead
and one woman
revived after a night with jordan
though pronounced dead on arrival
at st. paul's hospital
described jordan as
"a real decent-looking person
very mild-mannered
a real gentleman
he looked like a school teacher
white shirt and tie
I trusted him"

and in our situation in the downtown
    eastside
the single weapon we wield
like the weapon native indian prophets
like the weapon ancient hebrew
    prophets
used in situations of vicious
    displacement
and threatened destruction of their
    communities
was the word
words against the power
of money and law and politics and
    media
words against a global economic system
the word "hebrew" originally
    designated
not a racial class but a social class
of despised drifters and outcasts
who existed on the margins of middle

eastern cultures
and those advocates
those ancient hebrew prophets said

"the wealthy move the boundaries
and the poor have to keep out of the
    way
the poor spend the night naked, lacking
    clothes
with no covering against the cold
the child of the poor is exacted as
    security
from the city comes the groan of the
    dying
and the gasp of the wounded crying for
    help
damn those who destroy the huts of the
    poor
plundering their homes instead of
    building them up
those who tear the skin from off our
    people
who grind the faces of the poor
who join house to house
who add field to field
until there is room for no one but them
those who turn aside the way of the
    afflicted
who trample upon the oppressed"

and the native prophets of the americas
    who said

"when these times arrive
we will leave our homes like dying deer
the land will be sold and the people will
    be moved
and many things that we used to have
    in this land
will be taken from us
we have been made to drink
of the bitter cup of humiliation
they have taken away our lands

until we find ourselves fugitives,
    vagrants and strangers
in our own community
our existence as a distinct community
seems to be drawing to a close
our position may be compared
to a solitary tree in an open space
where all the forest trees around have
    been prostrated
by a furious tornado"

we have become a community of
    prophets
in the downtown eastside
rebuking the system
and speaking hope and possibility into
    situations
of apparent impossibility

a first nations man recently told me
he had come to the downtown eastside
    to die
he heard the propaganda
that this is only a place of death, disease
    and despair
and since his life had become a hopeless
    misery
he came here specifically to die
but he said
since living in the downtown eastside
what with the people he has met
and the groups he has found
he now wants very much to live

and his words go directly
to the heart of what makes for real
    community
a new life out of apparent death
and this is what we speak and live
with our words our weapons

our words
like bolts of lightning in a dark night

lighting our way
our words
like tears like rain like cries like hail
    from our hearts
feeling with each other in our suffering
    for each other
our words
angry as thunder exploding in the ears
    of those
who would ignore or dismiss or inflict
    upon us
what they in their ignorance think is
    best for us
our words defiant as streetkids in a
    cop's face
our words
brilliant and beautiful as the rainbow I
    saw
spanning our streets
our words
of resistance and comfort and
    commitment

like mountains
our words
prophetic on behalf of the hard-pressed
    poor
our words
buttons t-shirts fliers inserts
    newsletters pamphlets
posters spraypaint slogans stickers
    placards speeches
interviews essays poetry songs letters
    chalks paints
graffiti

for as one prophet said

"when all is dark the murderer leaves
    his bed
to kill the poor and oppressed"

our words

to block the murderers' paths

our words   spoken by

jeff and muggs and eldon and kathleen
    and frank and
maggie and carl and lori and duncan
    and margaret and
mark and sonny and ken and fred and
    sheila and liz
and tora and terri and ian and chris and
    bob and leigh
and jen and shawn and darren and
    sarah and irene and
cathy and ann and lorelie and nick and
    linda and john
and lorraine and joanne and judy and
    allison and sharon
and deb and marg and dan and jean and
    don and libby
and carol and lou and dayle and mo and
    barb and ellen

and sandy and tom and luke and gary
    and travis and
bruce and paul and deidre and jim and
    so many others

our words and our presence create
a strange and profound unity
outraged at each other
disappointing each other
misinterpreting each other
reacting against each other
resenting each other
unhealed wounds dividing us
when to be about unity
is to be caught in a crossfire
of conflicting ambitions understandings
    perspectives

still our words and our presence create
a strange and profound and strong
    unity
as in memory of the long hard nerve-
    wracking battles
for the carnegie centre
against the casino
for crab park
against brad holme
for zero displacement bylaws
against hotel evictions
for poor people living in woodward's
against condominium monstrosities
and for our very name
the downtown eastside
removed from city maps
the most stable community and
    neighbourhood
in vancouver   suddenly
    disappeared
but recovered through struggle
our name reclaimed but the meetings
    the pressure

the downtown eastside community

besieged and beleaguered
strung-out and dissipated
running on constant low-grade burn-
    out fever
meetings and meetings and meetings
a dozen fronts to fight at the same time
deal with one and a dozen more appear
another dehumanizing media story
or a new condo threat
a hundred needs crying out all at once
a hundred individuals with emergencies
crying for a response
sirens and sirens and sirens
construction noise
automobile mayhem
a disabled population
a poor and ill population
criminalized
up against globalization
pressure cooker emotional atmosphere
excruciating questions and dilemmas
so much happens so fast
how much compromise?
how to organize?
where to fight?
more sirens and screams and break-ins
welfare cuts
more murders and suicides
more bodies on the sidewalks and in
    alleys and parks
space and places for poor people
    shrinking
and the ambiguities of advocacy
the rumours
the well-founded paranoias
the political manipulations
exploitations confusions deliberate
    obfuscations
and seduction of the gentrification
    system
the backroom deals somewhere else
in office towers and government offices
meetings and more meetings

and yet
beneath the ostensible reason
for attending another goddamned
    meeting
is that which truly holds us together
holds and has held every real
    community together

love

love
not as passive abstraction or a
    commodity privatized
but love
as fiery personal and collective social
    justice passion
love as in our public celebrations
love as in our public grieving
love going past fatigue again
love taking risks in the face of
    uncertainty
love as stubbornness sticking to
    community principles
love as willingness to go one more
    length
to make one more leaflet
love sitting down together one more
    time
love saying hello to hate and fear and
    goodbye
love as resistance, tolerance and
    acceptance
love
for this poor beloved community
reeling from global upheavals
love
taking on the consequences of a system
    producing
more wounded
more damaged
more excluded
more refugees
more unemployed and never-to-be-

employed
and love's
immense capacity to care
and love as courage

like the other day near main and
    hastings
an old white man headed across
    hastings
in the middle of the block
traffic roared and blasted in both
    directions
the man was using a cane and moving
    very slowly
his eyes fixed somewhere beyond
it sure looked like he'd never make it
but would become
another vehicular maiming or death
    down here
and then a native fellow
waiting at the bus stop
like a matador dodging furious bulls
dodged into the traffic
and stopped it
using his body as a shield
and escorted the old white man
safely to the curb

words and courage and love and hope
    and unity
if only we had
the means for self-determination
instead

"the real estate cowboys . . . also
    enlisted the cavalry of
city government for . . . reclaiming the
    land and quelling
the natives, in its housing policy, drug
    crackdowns, and
especially in its parks strategy, the city
    devoted its
efforts not toward providing basic

services and living
opportunities for existing residents but
    toward routing
many of the locals and subsidizing
    opportunities for
real estate development"
wrote neil smith about the lower east
    side of new york

sounds familiar, literal
like the day the police showed up on
    horseback
to patrol the 100 block of east hastings
horses on the sidewalk
where some of the most ill and suffering
    human beings
most drugged and drunk and
    staggering human beings
slipped and stumbled through the huge
    horse turds
left laying on the sidewalk

I remember attending a kind of
    gentrification summit
called by a vancouver city planner
to examine the city's victory square
    redevelopment plan
david ley, jeff sommers, nick blomley,
    and chris olds
reached a similar conclusion
the plan does nothing to prevent
displacement and gentrification

but when recently reminded of this
   verdict
the city planner still pushing his plan
   said
"I don't care if god and david ley . . . "

and that's just it
the necessity for heeding
the prophetic blast and rallying cry
delivered by larry campbell
now the provincial coroner
in the carnegie centre last summer

"raise shit," he said

raise shit
against the kind of "urban cleansing"
gentrification unleashes
it's a war
against the poorest of the poor
1,000 overdose deaths
in the downtown eastside in 4 years
highest rate and number of suicides in
   vancouver
lowest life expectancy for both men and
   women
fatal epidemics of aids and hepatitis c
and lack of humane housing
identified as a major factor
in all this violence against us

raise shit
when a friend of mine, a gay native
   man, tells me
"I'll try anything to get a decent home
I'm gonna become a mental case
I'll even go into an institution if it'll
   help me
get a decent home"

raise shit
when both young people and hardcore
   addicts

either deliberately infect themselves
   with hiv or
take no precautions to prevent infection
   so that they
have a better chance at
obtaining housing, income, health care
   and meals

raise shit
when a city cop in a newspaper column
   says
"the locals were at their best fighting
   and howling"
and calls drug addicts "vampires"

raise shit
when an extremely influential north
   american
theoretician of displacement, george
   kelling
is brought to vancouver
by the business people and the police
to define and divide our community
   against itself
against panhandlers and prostitutes

raise shit
when a city planner in with the
   convention centre scam
says "the voters of vancouver can easily
   live with
20 to 25,000 homeless people and not
   even notice"

and when I think of raising shit
I think of this basketball team I once
   played on
composed of middle-aged beat-up
   alcoholics
and addicts from the streets
who'd been sober for awhile
and we entered a city recreational
   league

against teams that were
younger, stronger, faster, healthier and
    more skilled
and though we lost most games by a
    large margin
we determined that
no matter what the score
each hotshot team we played would
    know
by their fatigue and sweat and bruises
that they had been in a game
that they were up against an opponent
we knew we couldn't outjump or
    outrun those teams
but we sure could raise shit
better than they could
and amazingly we actually won a few
    games

to raise shit is to actively resist
and we resist with our presence
with our words
with our love
with our courage

we resist
person by person
square foot by square foot
room by room
building by building
block by block

we resist
because we are a community
of prophets, of activists, of advocates,
of volunteers, and agency workers
and we, you and I, us
are all that stands between

the unique vulnerable troubled life-
    giving and death-
attacked community of the downtown
    eastside

we are all that stands between our vast
    community
and those who would
gentrify and displace and replace it
replace with greed
the singular leadership we have here
where it is said we lack
a single dynamic individual leader
but we have
the most powerful leader there is
the most effective leader we can have
in this grave situation
our community
our community itself
has emerged as our leader
the downtown eastside community
    itself
leads us
and it is to our credit that this is so
for it is from our
prophetic, courageous, conflictual and
    loving
unity
that our community
raises shit
and resists

BUD OSBORN
2001

Words for the Last Page

This book marks the 16th birthday of the *Carnegie Newsletter*. The first edition was put together in a storage closet in the basement for Aug. 15, 1986 — 12 pages, 60 copies. It's been "that @O/oX#(*&A$ rag!" to 'the only paper I read from cover to cover every time!!" but the invisible victories are much deeper and more profound. The *Newsletter* has become a foundation for expression of universal principles, for gathering allies and propagating the ideology of justice. The Downtown Eastside is a microcosm of global struggles.

"In every living being there is a thirst for limitlessness"; the struggle is to progress without getting overcome with the sky-licking greed of humans, the impossibility of quenching this spiritual thirst with the desert of drugs and booze, money and power.

The dogmas of criminality and clean-up being identical are still dogma -bad theories presented as truth.

The prime directive is to elevate the dignity of women, a struggle expressed through building housing and a new Women's Centre, Breaking the Silence around violence against women, and the hidden obscenity of 59 missing women and the deaths of over 125 women in just a few years.

The prime directive is to raise the consciousness of humanity; the struggle to expose dark forces of gentrification, superiority complexes, forced dispersion of residents without concern for consequences and the driving greed and self-interest mistaken on purpose for enlightenment.

The *Carnegie Newsletter* is a pole in the spiritual magnet of the Downtown Eastside. All eyes are on us as the hub of a cosmic wheel, but our incredible strength is invisible, intangible, often incomprehensible. It is told to investors speculators and interested parties alike: "you have to talk to the community" — and it's fair notice. We are not vain-glorious, nor is anything exempt from the droll dabbling of dilettantes, but the networking and connections are invisible victories of enormous magnitude.

At the wild risk of whimsically willing a little wisp of wisdom to wing forth: *Baba Nam Kevalam — love is all there is.*

PAULR TAYLOR
VOLUNTEER EDITOR